Carriage Driving

The Crowood Press

First Published in 1988 by
The Crowood Press Ltd
Ramsbury, Marlborough
Wiltshire SN8 2HR
This impression 1996

British Library Cataloguing in Publication Data

Cowdery, John
Carriage driving.
1. Driving of horse-drawn vehicles
I. Title
798'.6 SF305

ISBN 1 85223 067 3

Dedication

This book is dedicated to my family who have cheerfully joined me in my chosen sport of carriage driving and who have been of great assistance in compiling this book.

Acknowledgements

The author would like to thank Miss Ishbel Chambers for information on the job of an event secretary described in Chapter 11.

Picture Credits

Figs 2 and 3 courtesy of John Parker; Figs 5, 6, 14, 18, 19, 22, 27, 35, 49, 50, 53, 58, 61, 63, 73, 75, 87, 91, 92, 97 and 108 by Leslie Lane; Figs 7, 8, 9, 10, 13, 16, 17, 21, 25, 30, 36, 37, 41, 42, 44, 51, 52, 55, 56, 57, 59, 60, 62, 68, 69, 70, 71, 72, 77, 78, 79, 81, 86, 88, 89, 90, 99, 100, 102, 103, 104, 105, 106, 107, 109, 110, 111, 112, 113, 114, 116, 118, 119, 123, 124, 125, 127, 130 and 132 by Ken Ettridge; Fig 12 by Anne Grossick; Fig 23 by Sandra Caton.

Line illustrations by Elaine How.

Typeset by Alacrity Phototypesetters, Weston-super-Mare
Printed and bound in Great Britain by WBC, Bridgend, Mid Glam.

Contents

1 The Sport's History

It is only human nature to be competitive, and history is full of tales of rivalry. Indeed, the first biblical story is of the competitiveness of Cain and Abel; it was only natural that as soon as man invented wheels he had to have a vehicle that was better and faster than his neighbours'. Stories of Greek and Roman chariot races liberally flavour the pages of ancient history, and the epic film *Ben Hur* has brought enjoyment and excitement to millions. Even in Britain there are tales of Queen Boadicea riding in her chariot at the head of her Iceni hordes to challenge the Roman invaders. The horse was the main motive power for such vehicles, and as tracks developed into roads and highways, so the war-like chariots and the later, lumbering stage wagons were superceded by a miscellany of coaches and carriages. With their sophistication came the better bred horse that was demanded for increased speed and durability. No sooner were the mail coach and passenger-carrying road coach introduced than the strong competitive spirit came once more to the fore and each tried to outdo the other for smartness, efficiency and speed.

The Beginnings of Competitive Driving

The British Driving Society

With the advent of the railways and then the motor car, new avenues of wheeled competition opened up and the horses and carriages went into a serious decline. Many vehicles were burnt or allowed to rot away to powdery wood and rusty iron, while others were consigned to the backs of barns and coach-houses to lie uncared-for and dust covered for many years. But as Europe emerged from the trauma of two world wars there was a resurgence of interest in horse-drawn vehicles spearheaded by Mr Sanders Watney, a keen member of the British Coaching Club who was later to become its President. With contemporaries like George Mossman, Tom Parker and Sir John Miller he breathed new life into the ailing club and as that once again flourished, he founded the British Driving Society to bring together those who had the interest and desire to drive horses and carriages to enjoy their sport.

Area Commissioners were appointed for the various counties of England, Scotland, Ireland and Wales and they were given the brief to organise instructional meets, picnic drives and similar events where driving enthusiasts could get together. This gave them the opportunity to compare notes, and learn from their own mistakes and from the mistakes of others so that the general standard of competence improved. Luckily there were a number of experienced people who gave freely of their time to advise areas and give instruction to their members on the correct way to harness-up and drive. Many of the smaller horse shows now started to introduce driving classes and became affiliated to the British Driving Society, which meant that all BDS members attending were given a black and yellow rosette. These rosettes were also distributed at every official meet and very soon harness rooms all over the country were displaying these distinctive trophies alongside the red, blue, yellow and green rosettes awarded in competition.

One of the most popular venues for drivers was the Royal Windsor Horse Show where, on the Sunday afternoon, an official BDS meet was held. After assembling on the showground they would drive through the beautiful Home Park, past the turreted walls of the Castle and along the well-mown banks of the River Thames. 'Sandy' Watney would lead the drive, usually with a pair of his versatile coach-horses harnessed to a phaeton or other such vehicle that he had found and lovingly restored. Many finds of that kind were being made as the BDS made carriage driving more popular and the demand for carriages, harness and suitable horses grew.

One man who was quick to appreciate the growing need for carriages was John Mauger of the auctioneering firm of Thimbley and Shorland. Very soon his Reading carriage sales became a Mecca for driving people, not only from Britain but also for enthusiasts from America and Europe who wanted some of the vehicles that John Mauger and his team were unearthing. Collections that had lain undiscovered in barns and outbuildings now saw the light of day as their owners found that there was a market for them at Reading. Not only vehicles and harness, but a myriad of driving bric-à-brac found its way on to the auctioneer's floor in those early years, and is still doing so, although the chances of picking up a bargain are not as great as they used to be. The complete Brougham fore-carriage that was sold fairly cheaply in the early days of the sales would now command a three-figure price. Two well-known driving enthusiasts, George Bowman and Jack Collinson saw their investment in a coach they had initially thought expensive appreciate by ten times in only a few years. Indeed, many people who bought carriages in the 1960s and early 1970s have found that their investment has been worth while.

So the British Driving Society grew and flourished to become, as it is today, the backbone of show driving in Britain. Indeed, it has many members in other countries of the world whose driving is guided by the newsletters and journals that the society regularly sends out. In the mid-1960s, in the United States of America, the Carriage Association of America was formed, to be followed in 1974 by the American Driving Society, whose aims were similar to its British forerunner. As had happened in Britain, the society also became the adviser to many shows who now wanted to run driving classes, as well as organising picnics, marathons and shows of its own. At first most turn-outs were of the four-wheeled American buggy type, but as the American Driving Society's popularity grew, more people discovered that a two-wheeled vehicle was more suitable for a

Fig 1 Tommy Fawcett at Lowther Park, 1983.

show ring. Coach builders specialising in these vehicles were soon doing a brisk trade.

Of course all countries have had their own various styles of horse transport, and in the 1960s this was still very much in evidence in the Eastern-Bloc countries of Europe where agriculture was still largely dependent on the horse; and the state-controlled studs included driving in their curricula. Some of these studs held local shows, but the largest driving events at that time were in West Germany at Aachen and Hamburg.

International Competition

It was at the latter in 1969 that the then President of the Fédération Equestre Internationale, HRH Prince Philip, first saw four-in-hands from Germany and Hungary competing. Having had a discussion at a previous FEI meeting with the Polish delegate, Eric Brabec, about the possibility of creating an international competition for carriages, he now saw that this could be feasible. Consequently, on his return to England, he contacted Col. Mike Ansell who was a senior member of the FEI Bureau and a well-known organiser of equestrian events, and persuaded him to devise a driving competition. Mike Ansell had no experience whatsoever of driving, but he knew the right people to help him and these he got together in Berne, Switzerland to work on the suggestion put forward by the Duke of Edinburgh and Eric Brabec. The British expert at the time was Bernard Mills, son of the famous circus proprietor Bertram Mills, who had himself been an ardent coachman, running the 'Old Times' coach from London to Brighton, and assembling a collection of coaches which included the Wells Fargo Concord which had been brought to this country by Col. 'Buffalo Bill' Cody. Bernard had for many years been a member of the Coaching Club and was a respected judge of horses and carriages of all types, so was a natural choice to spearhead the formation of the new sport in Britain.

Rules

The rules that were drawn up in Berne were kept as simple as possible and outlined a competition based, in principle, on the ridden three-day event. On the first day the drivers were to do a dressage test, as the riders did in their competition A, with the difference that the carriages would first have an inspection. Their competition A was therefore divided into A(I) Presentation and A(II) Dressage. The second day was to be a cross-country competition in much the same vein as the ridden event and similarly divided into sections. There were to be five sections, A to E:

A First, a trot section along roads and tracks.
B A walk section of about one kilometre.
C After a halt of ten minutes, a further trot section, in which was included a maximum of eight man-made or natural obstacles for the driver to negotiate.
D Another walk section and ten-minute halt.
E The final trot section similar to the first.

Each section was allotted maximum and minimum times in which it was to be driven and penalty points were awarded for being outside these times. In section C, the obstacles, or hazards as they were termed, each had an optimum time in which they were to be driven, with a maximum time limit of five minutes, after which the competitor was deemed to be eliminated and should then withdraw from the hazard and that phase of the competition.

The final day, on which the ridden eventers have showjumping, was to be a test of driving skill through a series of pairs of cones laid out in the show ring, to prove that both horses and drivers had come unscathed through the previous day's competition and still retained the discipline and accuracy of driving. From this phase of the competition what we now know as scurry driving developed, where pairs of ponies excite the crowds at major horse shows by racing round a similar cone course.

When the rules for this new sport were formulated by that knowledgeable band of men assembled by Mike Ansell in Switzerland, potential competitors and event organisers read them avidly and the sport was soon attracting new drivers. Some of these tended to copy the example set by the established competitors without bothering to make themselves really conversant with the rules. This is a very slipshod way of learning and eventually leads to the competitor falling foul of some technicality.

As any sport progresses, its rules are being continually updated and carriage driving is no exception. Those whose job it is to keep the rules up to date make every effort to ensure that they are simple and very much to the point.

The original rules governing the three-day competition have obviously undergone many revisions since they were devised and are still under constant review by the Driving Committee of the FEI which is the sport's governing body. In Britain there is a set of national rules drawn up by the Horse Driving Trials Group of the British Horse Society and based on the FEI rules. However, the FEI rules only refer to competitions for teams of four horses, and in Britain there are events for singles, pairs and tandems so there must also be special conditions applicable to each of these types of turn-out. Not only that, but there are also classes for ponies in each of these divisions, yet another dimension that has to be taken into consideration.

Although there is a constant update of the rules, the most important part is never changed and that is the preamble which says:

'These rules ... should be interpreted with intelligence and in the spirit of the sport. In any unforeseen and exceptional circumstances, it is the duty of the jury to make a decision in a sporting spirit and approaching as nearly as possible the intention of these rules.'

Looking back at some of those early rules, they now appear to have a simple naïvety of which cunning competitors were quick to take advantage, bringing hasty amendments from red-faced officials. For instance, it was realised that there were fewer penalties for breaking pace and cantering through the walk section than would be incurred for being over the time allowed. That was soon rectified, and now anyone caught deliberately breaking pace in the walk sections is eliminated.

The term elimination requires some explanation. If, for some reason, a competitor is eliminated in any phase of the competition, A(I), A(II), B or C, he is allowed to continue with the remainder of the competition, and may even be fortunate enough to win one of the other phases, but in the final assessment he will be placed after all those in his class who have not been eliminated. If he retires voluntarily, then, in the final placing, he will come after those who have been eliminated. In both cases they receive penalty points for the competition in which they were eliminated or retired and these are calculated by taking the score of the competitor who finished with the most penalty points and adding on a further 25 per cent of that score.

As the rules have become more explicit, eliminations have become rarer and the emphasis has always been on making the competition as fair as possible for all drivers. This has also meant an increase in the number of officials required to oversee and assist at the events. Initially there were only one or two judges on the marathon hazards, but now the normal number is four and electronic timing equipment is also being used, all in an effort to ensure that everyone is given the fairest possible chance.

Competitive Driving Events

Once the rules had been formulated, events began to be organised, and the Swiss were the first to get the wheels rolling, in a manner of speaking, with an event at Lucerne in 1970. Britain was quick to follow suit and the next year the

Royal Windsor Horse Show was persuaded to incorporate an International Driving Grand Prix. Sir John Miller, the Crown Equerry in charge of the Royal Mews, was already an enthusiastic member of the Coaching Club, and at Prince Philip's suggestion eagerly tried his hand at this new form of four-horse driving. His lead was quickly followed by other members of the Club, Douglas Nicholson, George Mossman and John Richards who together with the leading lady whip, Mrs Cynthia Haydon and that sporting character Mr John Parker got the sport off to a good start in Britain.

European and World Championships

The first European Championships were organised by the Hungarians in Budapest later that year; and then, in 1972, the first World Driving Championships were held in Munster, West Germany. Although August Dubey of Switzerland won the individual gold medal, Sir John Miller's silver and Douglas Nicholson's bronze meant that Britain won the team gold medal.

The pattern was now set that there were to be European Championships one year and World Championships the next, a format which was to hold until 1985, when the European Championships were discontinued and replaced by a World Championship for pairs of horses. There is now a European Championship for Pony Teams and the prospect of future championships being arranged for Single Horses.

Fig 2 John Parker in the 1976 World Championships at Apeldoorn, Holland.

Fig 3 The 1979 European Championships at Haras du Pin, France: John Parker driving.

Fig 4 George Bowman with his cob team at Frauenfeld, 1972.

National Events in Britain

While Royal Windsor Horse Show continues to be the annual international event held in Britain, many other national events have grown up over the years. One of the first was held at Lowther, in Cumbria, and it was here that Prince Philip made his début as a driver in 1973. Beamish was also an early venue, but while Lowther continues to flourish, Beamish has unfortunately been dropped from the driving calender. The sport has been very lucky in that many large estates have consented to run an event and in appreciation of this privilege competitors make every effort to do as little damage as possible to such historic properties as Cirencester Park, Floors Castle, Goodwood and, of course, Windsor Great Park.

Since 1975 there have been National Championships in Britain for all classes

Fig 5 Sarah Garnett and her first tandem at Kelso, 1981.

Fig 6 Karen Bassett driving her mother's team of Shetlands at Kelso, 1981.

from singles to teams, and after being held firstly at Cirencester and then at Goodwood they finally settled in Windsor, as the most suitable place for the most prestigious competition. For the last ten years, these championships have been sponsored by Famous Grouse Whisky, and in 1983 they also agreed to sponsor a national competition for novice drivers. While the final for this novice competition is held in conjunction with the National Championships, the qualifying rounds take place at both national and club events during the year. More and more of these qualifying events are now held at the driving clubs which have been formed throughout the country over the past fifteen years and which are presently going from strength to strength. These clubs hold both social and competitive events and are ideal venues for anyone beginning to drive. Most of them are organised by people who have a wealth of experience in both show driving and the FEI competitions, and are only too willing to help and encourage others. Most of these clubs are affiliated to the Driving Trials Group of the British Horse Society (*see* Useful Addresses).

2 Horses and Ponies

Everyone has their own reason for starting carriage driving. It may be something that has always appealed to you, or you may have become interested in it by helping a friend with their turn-out, or you may have been watching others compete and now feel that you would like to try your hand at it. There are many different reasons why people begin, but one of the most common is that the family pony, who has been an excellent servant to the growing youngsters, is no longer wanted for pony clubs and local gymkhanas, as the pull of the teenage social life leads them to discover new pleasures and they are spending more time on school work as important examinations have to be tackled. So what are Mum and Dad to do with the four-legged friends with whom no one can bear to part? Driving seems to be the logical answer, as the age of the driver does not have to be so compatible with the size of the animal as when it is shown under saddle.

The next step is to decide what sort of driving should be contemplated. Although most driving ponies are capable of doing most things that are asked of them, it is very necessary to adopt a 'horses for courses' attitude when intending to compete in horse driving trials at national or even international level. The Horse Driving Trials Group has now set a standard of weights and track widths that governs the sizes of carriages in events and it is really unfair for a large person to burden a small pony not only with his weight but also with that of the groom. (A competitor is obliged to have a groom riding in the carriage with him as they cover several phases of cross-country going which can vary from leg-punishing hardness to deep glutinous mud.) If the pony is really not up to that then you must content yourself with finding your driving enjoyment at the excellent meets and shows organised by driving societies. If he is strong and active, however, and still sufficiently young to cope with an event – and most ponies that have endured youthful riders are fairly tough and resilient – you are well away and now have only the problem of turning that much loved riding pony into a competent driving animal. If you are not blessed with the time or experience to do this, it is far better to have the conversion made by an expert trainer whose reputation for turning out safely schooled carriage horses can be relied upon.

Buying a Driving Horse

Presuming that you do not already have the pony or horse and are, therefore, free to choose, there is a very wide range of possibilities. Your choice will obviously be governed by your own size, as it would look ridiculous for a large man to drive too small a pony, or for a petite lady to try to manage a seventeen-hand giant. So, due regard must be given to the overall effect that your turn-out will have on a judge. The price is also important because, although you want the best that you can possibly afford, you must also remember that you have the additional cost of the vehicle and harness to enable you to compete. Once the initial outlay for these items has been dealt with it is always possible to change your horse or pony for something more expensive if, by that time, you have not become too attached to him.

Important Characteristics

What is important in a driving horse? Most of the advertisements that you see will tell you that a horse is safe to box, clip and shoe, and these considerations are of course most important. If you are travelling to shows or events there is nothing worse than spending a long time trying to persuade a stubborn animal to get into a horse-box or trailer. The scene usually draws a crowd of helpful 'experts' who will all tell you what you should have done to get him loaded, when all that you need to have done was to see him loaded before you bought him. This is all part of that important necessity – the right temperament. This rather undefinable quality can soon be assessed as you watch a prospective purchase being put through his paces. He should stand quietly while his harness is put on and walk easily out of the stable to be put to the vehicle. When asked to move off with the vehicle the quiet acceptance of the preparation should then be galvanised into brisk action and a willing response to the driver's command. One useful tip at this point is always to watch the vendor driving the horse before you are persuaded to take the reins yourself. It may seem an obvious precaution, but most accidents happen when driving a horse who belongs to someone else and experiences a different hand on the reins.

There is quite a prejudice against the use of mares for driving because they are more liable to kick than geldings and can also be difficult when in season, but I have driven several mares and found that if they were properly schooled they were as reliable as their male counterparts. If a mare is liable to be difficult it will soon become apparent as you watch the crupper being fitted under her tail. If she strongly resents this, and even tries to kick at the groom, she is definitely a miss who should be missed.

For your first driving horse you should buy something that is not too young and has a certain amount of experience. Obviously young horses are cheaper but they require experienced hands to give them the necessary tuition. A driving horse's prime years are from four to ten years and it is in that age range that the price is highest, but animals who have been well looked after can have a useful driving life well past this point. Imre Abonyi, who was World Champion in 1976, was quoted as saying that he preferred to drive a team of twelve-year-olds, as by that age they were sensible and sure of the job that they were required to do. So don't let a bit of age put you off a horse who seems suitable in all other respects. How long he lasts will largely be up to you, depending on how you use and care for him.

Accommodation

A great deal in horse care depends on how much time the horse will be kept in the stable and how much he will be out in the field. If, by force of circumstance, he will have to spend a considerable amount of the time outside, you will be well advised to choose a sturdy native breed who will grow a sufficiently long coat to give him the necessary insulation against a changeable climate. If you have never looked after a horse before it might be an advantage, at least for the first year, to keep him at a livery stable, where you will see what attention he requires and learn about diet and stable management. Most of this can be learned from books but there are little quirks and ways of doing things that only come by experience. There is a lot of truth in the saying that 'fools learn by their own mistakes and wise men from the experience of others'.

Presuming that you have decided to keep the horse at a livery stable, it is important to ascertain that they will have a space for him before you buy him. It will also be an advantage if they have somewhere for you to keep your carriage, as it will save you the bother of trailing it there every time you want to go for a drive. Having taken all these considerations to heart, it is now time to decide which of the many breeds of driving horse will be suitable for you.

Breeds

Welsh

This is by far the most popular breed of competition driving pony and horse. There are four basic sections to this

Fig 7 Mrs Jill Holah driving her Welsh pony Coed Coch Pippin.

breed, each governed by height. Those in Section A are the smallest ponies and include any under 12 hh. They are stylish in appearance, looking rather like miniature Arabs and moving with the same easy, flowing action. They look very impressive in the dressage arena and can be fast through the hazards, but their size really limits their use to lightweight ladies, unless they are used in pairs or teams when they will be pulling a four-wheeled vehicle and will not have the weight of a single vehicle on their backs. Section B is for ponies between 12 and 13 hh. who are not quite so fine as their smaller brethren. They tend to look more like Section C, who are more cob-like, with a high knee action and a thicker set appearance. At the top of the Welsh line are the Section D cobs. There is no height limit but these are usually best around the 15 hh. mark. They are smart, sturdy and strong, with silky feathers which accentuate their extravagant action. This eye-catching movement is an advantage in dressage and their sturdiness carries them well through the rigorous marathon section. George Bowman was most successful with his first team of Welsh cobs and became British National Champion in his first season with them.

Shetland

These hairy, rugged ponies, who have been made famous by the cartoonist Thelwell, are strong, willing and fast. Though these attributes are excellent

Fig 8 John Bowman driving his Welsh cob stallion Lockeridge Timothy.

Fig 9 Sue and Ken Jackson enjoying a drive with their Shetland tandem.

when tackling hazards, they do not make them good dressage ponies. They have been most successful when driven in pairs and teams, with their speed and small size particularly suiting them to scurry competitions (*see* Chapter 10).

Dartmoor

One of the smallest of British native breeds, they are usually about 12 hh. They make good driving ponies but, due to their size, have only been successful in competition when in pairs or teams.

Fig 10 Pippa Basset driving her mother's team of Dartmoor ponies at Wylye.

New Forest

A slightly larger pony who is suitable for driving, although not very 'showy'. If considering buying one of these it is best to contact the New Forest Pony Society to ensure that you get the genuine article because some well-meaning people introduced some alien stallions to the forest some years ago which led to cross-breeding.

Exmoor

A good strong pony who has had considerable success in driving. He is noticeable for the mealy markings around his mouth.

Fell

By far the most successful driving pony in competition at present. This sturdy

Fig 11 The author's daughter, Debbie, driving the Fell mare Dene Betony Blossom.

pony, who was bred for pack and draught work in northern England, has the strength and stamina necessary for gruelling cross-country competitions. Though basically not a dressage pony, if the training is started early enough these willing ponies will learn to master the differing paces and movements required to perform a perfectly respectable test.

Dales

The larger counterpart of the Fell pony, a Dales is between 14 hh. and 14.2 hh. (the maximum height for ponies). Dales have also been widely used for driving, mainly in the North-east of England which is the home territory of the breed. Although some have been used in the three-day events, they are most popular with the farmers and tradesmen for the light trade turn-outs seen at many shows.

Arabs

Although the pure Arab is not a suitable driving horse, some part-bred Arabs have been successfully broken to harness and shown in private driving classes. To be classed as a part-bred the horse must have 12 per cent pure Arab blood, that is, one great-grandparent, or two great-great-grandparents, and the other 88 per cent can be any other breed. It is this larger percentage that will determine his suitability for driving. Part-breds have yet to prove themselves at three-day events and can be rather too sharp for the novice to handle.

Fig 12 Griselda MacDonald with her Hackney pony Kippen Kaimsman.

Hackney

This is the most stylish carriage horse, having a high-stepping, flashy action. Mrs Cynthia Haydon drove a team of Hackney horses in the early days of FEI driving and was a member of the British team. Since then a few Hackney horses have been driven singly, as well as Hackney ponies in pairs, always with great success. However, this breed is also very sharp and quick thinking and requires a driver who is fairly expert – not really suitable for a novice.

Cleveland Bay

One of the oldest breeds in Britain and ideally suited to all types of carriage work. Although a pure Cleveland is rather large, around 16.2 hh. plus, for competitive driving, they have been successfully crossed with lighter horses to produce excellent competition horses. HRH Prince Philip has been most successful with a team of Cleveland cross Oldenburg horses which, although they strongly resemble pure Clevelands, are slightly lighter in the legs and, consequently, have better paces.

Hanoverian

A German carriage horse similar in stamp to the Cleveland Bay but comes in a greater variety of colours. When the ruling house of England was the House of Hanover, the state coach was drawn by a team of Hanoverian Creams but when, during the First World War, the

Fig 13 HRH Prince Michael of Kent driving a pair of Cleveland Bays at Holker Hall, 1986.

Fig 14 HRH The Duke of Edinburgh driving a team of Cleveland Bays at Wramplingham, 1982.

name of the royal house was changed to Windsor, the Hanoverian Creams were disposed of and replaced by grey horses who were then called the Windsor Greys.

Lippizaner

The most famous of the Hungarian breeds, the Lippizaner has been very successful in carriage driving competitions. Gyorgy Bardos won the World Championships with a team of Lippizaner stallions in 1978 and 1980. They are intelligent animals who respond well to training and have a showy action combined with speed across country.

Hungarian

Many varieties of carriage horse come from Hungary but they are all basically rather lean, leggy animals whose main attribute is their ability to cover the ground very quickly. Many of the strains have Lippizaner blood somewhere along the line, which gives style to these very successful competition horses.

Trakehner

This Polish breed of horse has been quite successful for the Poles in international competition and is one of the best looking

Fig 15 George Bowman with his Lippizaner team at the World Championships in Szilvasvarad, Hungary, 1984.

Fig 16 Lex Ruddiman with his team of Hungarian bred horses.

of the Continental breeds. The breeding is carefully controlled by the State and the horses are only sold to foreigners with reluctance. Even then it is not always possible to get the best of the studs.

Oldenburg

Another useful German carriage horse which Col. Sir John Miller popularised in Britain by introducing the breed into the Royal Mews and successfully crossing it with the Cleveland Bays.

Gelderlander

This smart, upstanding Dutch horse has an extravagant action and is heavy boned. When coaching was on the upsurge in the 1950s, George Matthey brought several teams over to Britain and was very successful with them in coaching marathons. His example was soon copied by Douglas Nicholson, who drove a team of Gelderlanders in the first World Championships at Munster in 1972. The most recent success for these horses was in the hands of Peter Munt, who drove a team belonging to Norman Smith, to win the British National Championships at Harrogate in 1986. Being big, strong horses they require firm and expert handling and are not really suitable for a novice.

Dutch Warmblood

Another smart breed of Dutch horse, they are a little lighter than Gelderlanders or Friesians. Warmbloods are bred and driven successfully by Tjerd Velstra, who has twice been World Champion, and also by his brilliant pupil Ijsbrand Chardon.

Fig 17 Peter Munt driving Mr N. D. B. Smith's Gelderlander team – National Champions 1986.

Fig 18 Tjerd Velstra driving his team of Dutch Warmbloods at Windsor, 1983.

Friesian

A high-actioned Dutch breed, usually black in colour and having heavily feathered legs. In the nineteenth century Friesians were in great demand as funeral horses because of their imposing presence and impressive action. Tjerd Velstra drove a team of Friesians to win the International Driving Grand Prix at the Royal Windsor Horse Show in 1974 and, although he has changed his allegiance, there are still several Friesian teams being regularly used in competition.

Swedish Warmblood

Although used successfully by the Pahlsson brothers, those Swedish Warmbloods that were brought to Britain have met with varying success. The first team was imported by Stig Gorrel and these have been moderately successful, but other horses brought over by Peter Munt never worked really well as carriage horses. Mark Weston used Swedish Warmbloods in the 1986 World Championships, where he was the highest placed British competitor, but he was never very happy with these horses who are fairly fine-legged and susceptible to laminitis when used on consistent hard going.

Irish

These honest horses are not particularly showy and their action is not outstanding but they are amenable to most jobs and make excellent driving horses. When fashion has led the more affluent to buy Hungarian or Dutch horses, the Irish

Fig 19 Nicci Pahlson driving his team of Swedish Warmbloods at Brighton, 1987.

Fig 20 Lt.-Col. Hopkinson of the Royal Horse Guards driving a pair of Irish Greys, 1968.

have rather taken a back seat but they are still in the majority in the various types of driving in Great Britain. They are easy to train and most are quite unflappable when in a tight spot. They are usually quite reasonably priced and a good choice for a newcomer to driving or particularly to competitive driving.

The Suitable Horse

Having decided what breed would suit you best there is now the choice of the actual animal, and in every breed they still come in varying shapes and sizes. Perfection in animals is about as rare as it is in humans but it is still something to be desired. You can tell a lot about a horse just by looking him straight in the eye, and you will soon know if it is a friendly gaze or a malevolent glare that greets you. As you look at the horse he should be standing well, with his weight evenly distributed over each of his four legs so that he is standing on a rectangle and not resting any of his feet inside or outside that imaginary oblong. When viewed from the side his legs and body should form a box as long as it is high. This will not apply to horses under four years old, where the withers and quarters may be at different heights as the horse has not finished growing. While still looking at the side of the horse you should also note the topline, which is the silhouette from the ears to the tail. This should divide into three parts:

1. From the ears to the withers.
2. From the withers to the loins.
3. From the loins to the tail.

The first two should be equal in length and the third should be three-quarters of one of these measurements. The quarters should be well-rounded and muscled to give plenty of driving power when you ask your horse to lean into his collar for a difficult pull.

A good driving horse should have a deep girth which should be at least half the distance from withers to the ground. The shoulders should not be too upright but slope backwards at an approximate angle of 45 degrees. This will accommodate a full collar comfortably, still allowing the horse to move freely.

The legs are important in any horse but are especially so for a driving horse as you will be pounding him along Tarmac roads for a great deal of time. If you run your hand down his forelegs below the knee you will find that there are two bones, a larger one in front called the cannon bone and a smaller one running parallel behind it. Between these two run the bundle of nerves and tendons that operate the forelegs. Any lump or protrusion on either of these bones will rub those tendons and soon cause lameness so this is obviously to be avoided.

Everyone knows that you tell the age of the horse by his teeth (a fact which

Fig 21 Andrew Mylius driving his pair of Highland ponies.

Fig 22 Mary Basset's team of English spotted ponies at Brighton, 1984.

gave rise to the saying that you never look a gift horse in the mouth) but, if you are not sure how to read the dental markings and do not believe the vendor, it is best to get your vet to check the age for you. In any case, as you are spending a considerable amount of money on the horse, it is worth while to lay out a few more pounds for a veterinary report on the animal.

When you have had a good look around the horse while he is standing still (and he should stand still during your inspection – you do not want a fidget), you now want to see him move. He should be trotted up for you without harness so that you can study his action. He should move freely with a smooth, not jerky, motion and cover the ground in easy strides. Watch him trot towards you and away from you and check that he does so in a straight line, without crossing his legs, 'plaiting', or scooping his feet outwards – an action known as 'dishing'. A lot can be learned from the position of the horse's head as he trots along. He should hold it proudly in front of him with his ears upright and pointed forward in an attentive attitude. His neck should be bent just behind the ears but not over-bent, which indicates that mechanical devices have been excessively employed in holding his head in.

Having had a good look over the horse and seen him move, it is time to see him work. It is worth repeating that it is important to see how the horse accepts the harness being put on and then stands still while he is put in the shafts. When asked to move off he should lean into his collar and move straight forward. When asked to turn he should come round in a smooth arc, turning his head in the direction in which he is to go, maintaining a forward movement, and not trying to move sideways in a crab-like action. He should go uphill and downhill with the same ease, showing that he is not bothered by either collar or breeching.

By this point it should be apparent to you whether or not he is a suitable animal for you, and if you can already drive you should now take the reins yourself; if you are not too proficient, however, it is better to take a trusted friend who is capable of making this final assessment for you.

3 Harness

The Evolution of Harness

It was about two thousand years before the birth of Christ that oxen were first yoked up to pull vehicles. This early method of attaching an animal to a vehicle was simply a shaped wooden bar or yoke which rested on the ox's neck and to which the pole of the vehicle was attached. When the ponderous ox was replaced by the faster horse, the yoke was still used but was now assisted by a breast strap and trace to pull the vehicle along.

The next step was to attach a strap to hold the yoke in place and the yoke was moved from the horse's neck to his back so that the strap could go round his barrel in the form that we would now recognise as a girth. Because it was found that the breast strap has a tendency to slip up and press on the horse's windpipe, a strap was attached to the centre of the breast strap, passed down between the front legs and tied to the girth in the same manner as the modern-day breastplate. It was only common sense to put a pad under the yoke to give the horse greater comfort and it was in this form that chariot harness for pairs of horses was to continue for hundreds of years.

The first use of shafts is attributed to the Chinese and they also introduced a basic form of breeching. It was in China too that a form of collar was introduced, later to be copied by the Romans who travelled extensively by horse-drawn chariots and other vehicles throughout their empire. That covered most of Western Europe and it can be seen how their ideas on harness were copied and improved upon, with different styles of the same basic idea being developed.

Leather has always been found to be the most suitable material for making harness and even with the advent of today's webbing harness, which requires very little maintenance, a set of leather harness still looks better and is more convenient to use. Although the methods of producing harness leather, by tanning with oak bark, have changed little over the years, modern processes ensure a more consistent result and the harness maker consequently can rely on all the hides he receives being of a similar high quality. Patent leather is used for collar covering, pad tops and blinkers, and this was originally made by several smoothings of the leather surface followed by a process known as japanning or varnishing. Today such leathers are finished with a polyurethane which is less likely to crack but makes the leather rather more difficult to mould into shape. Other modern harness-making methods include the filling of collars with a semi-hard foam instead of the usual straw and replacing metal blinker plates with lighter ones made of fibreglass. Saddle trees for single harness used to be made of solid wood which was liable to split, but the use of modern laminates makes this less likely to happen.

There are several styles of harness depending on use and the size of the horse. For instance, the harness used on a heavy horse is much more robust than that which is suitable for carriage horses. The trade turn-out and harness is very similar to that of the private driving horse, but because of its commercial use it needs to be slightly heavier and much stronger. Carriage horses used for ceremonial processions have a much more ornate harness, although basically similar. In America, where trotting racing is a very popular sport, a light type of harness suitable for this purpose is used. This is known as 'fine harness' and the carriage harness is therefore sometimes referred to as 'heavy harness' in order to distinguish it from the other type.

Single Harness

The two basic types of single harness differ only by virtue of the different types of collar used and are, therefore, known as full collar harness or breast collar harness. In full collar harness the collar is fitted around the horse's neck whereas the breast collar is simply a broad strap across the horse's chest, held up by another strap over the neck. The advantage of the full collar is that it covers a greater area of the horse's shoulder and therefore allows him to exert a greater pull than on the single breast collar. However, the latter is a lot lighter and more suited to cross-country driving, giving the horse greater freedom of movement, which is an asset when negotiating tricky hazards. The full collar can be attached to either roller bolts or swingletrees, but because a breast collar allows the extra movement of the shoulders, it must be attached to a swingletree to avoid rubbing the horse's shoulders.

The full collar should preferably be

Fig 23 American-style trotters in fine harness.

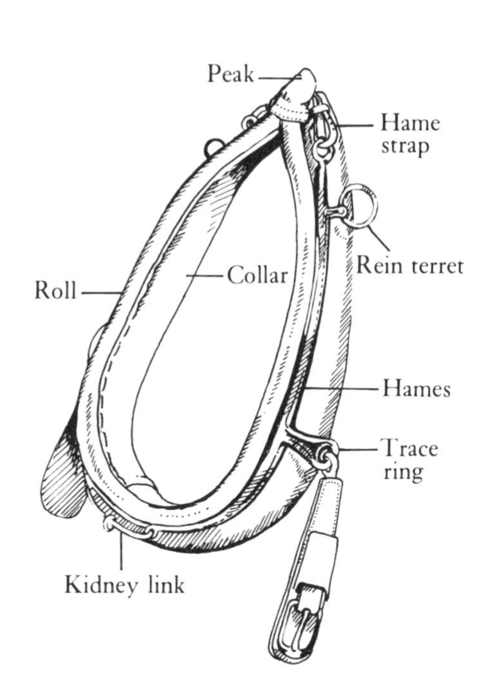

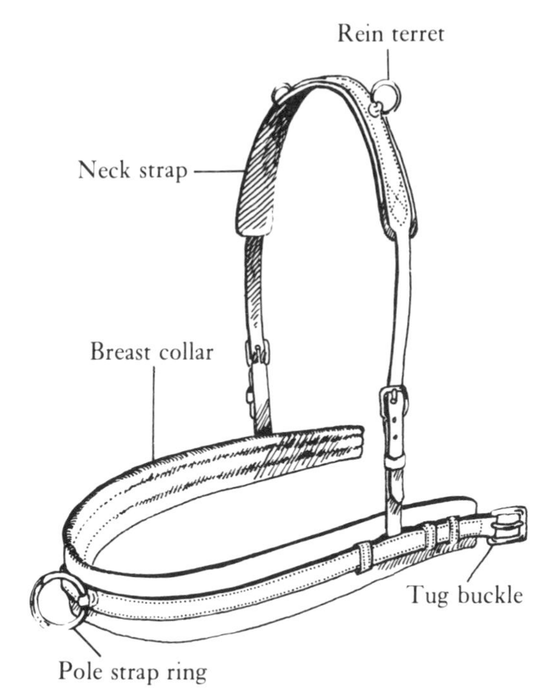

Fig 24 Full collar and breast collar.

made especially for the horse as a good fit is essential. It should lay evenly down the shoulder and there should be enough room at the bottom end for a clenched fist to be inserted by the windpipe. This is to ensure that no matter how hard the horse leans into the collar, his breathing will not be restricted. Breathing is also the major consideration when fitting a breast collar because this should be straight across the horse's chest, not too high to press against the windpipe nor too low to interfere with the action of the forelegs. If a breast collar is used for wheelers or pair horses, a neck strap should also be used, especially if there is no breeching. This is to enable the horse to hold back on the pole head without slipping completely through his harness. Artillery gun teams all use breast collars and the horses alongside the pole wear neck straps as well as breeching, in order to control the heavy guns and limbers as they gallop through the intricate movements of a musical drive.

The traces buckle straight into the end of a breast collar but a full collar is fitted with a pair of metal hames to which the traces are attached. These hames used to be made of steel and had a layer of brass casing applied to them. Modern casting techniques enable a strong brass and bronze alloy to be used but they are not quite as strong as the steel ones which can still be found on some carefully preserved sets of harness.

Collar

As part of the hames you have a rein terret about six inches (15cm) from the

Fig 25 Bronwyn Johnson driving a pony in breast collar harness.

top of the hame and about ten inches (25cm) below that (more or less depending on the size of collar being used) is the hames arm on to which the shoulder piece is attached. This shoulder piece consists of a metal loop which passes through the hames arm and has long ends which are riveted on to strong pieces of leather. To these are sewn the tug buckles into which the traces will go; behind the tug buckle there is usually a flap of leather known as a 'safe' and the trace should pass through this before going through the buckle. This lessens the wear on the trace as it acts as a pad between the buckle and the trace. A strong hames strap holds the two hames together and this is fastened securely across the top or peak of the collar. The spare end of the strap should always point to the off side so that if any adjustment is needed, it can most easily be done from the near side without having to stand dangerously in the middle of the road.

The end fitting for single harness traces used in showing and driving competition is the tapered slot. There should be two such slots in the end of the trace, the one nearest to the end of the trace being hooked on to the vehicle. This leaves the spare slot available for use should the working slot become torn. The trace should be sufficiently long and have enough holes at the front end to allow such adjustment to be made without interfering with the position of the horse in the shafts. On light trade and commercial harness, chain ends are used on the traces which are more practical for everyday use as the links do not wear in the way that leather slots would. The chain also allows considerable adjustment to be made and consequently this type of trace is usually sewn directly on to the hames.

Pads

The saddle pad used in single harness is a most important item because it supports the shafts of the vehicle and must, therefore, be of strong construction and comfortable for the horse to wear. The basis of its manufacture is a wooden tree with a metal channel through which the back band can pass. The tree is covered in leather through which the two rein terrets are screwed. The long leather side panels or skirts of the pad are usually shaped to provide a wider area where the shaft tugs will rest. If the pad is too small for the horse, the tugs will be below the wide area and catch against the girth. The underside of the pad should be well stuffed to allow a clear channel above the horse's backbone. There is a 'D' at the back of the pad top for attaching the crupper back strap, and if the stuffing is insufficient, or has become too flat, this 'D' is likely to press uncomfortably into the backbone with damaging results.

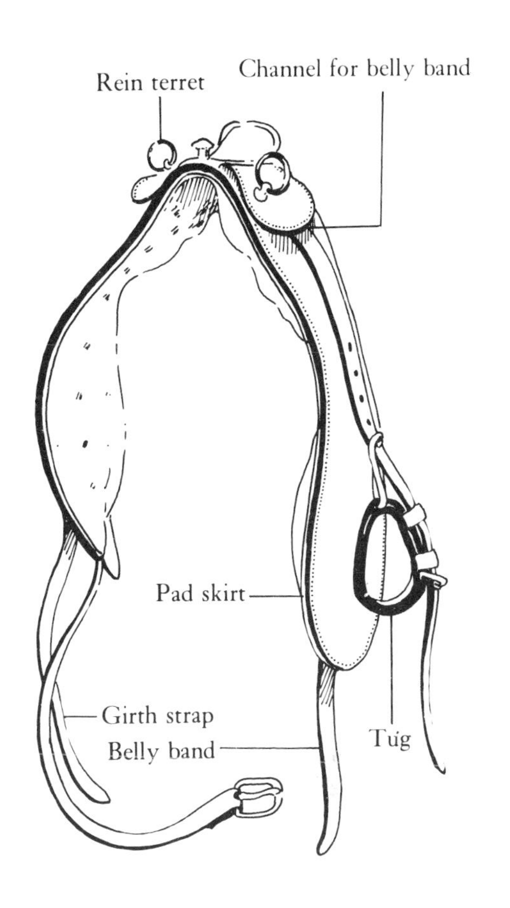

Fig 26 Saddle pad for single harness.

Girths

The girth should be fastened sufficiently tightly to prevent the pad from slipping sideways on the horse's back. The back band which supports the shaft tugs should be fastened when the horse is in the shafts and should allow the shaft tugs a slight movement up and down to facilitate the balance of the vehicle. The tugs are made in a variety of patterns but the most usual type are oval in shape through which the shafts slip easily. If the vehicle being used is a four-wheeler with

Fig 27 Lady Hugh Russell driving a four-wheeled single vehicle using Tilbury tugs.

independent shafts, a Tilbury tug must be used which is in the form of a 'U'-shaped metal cup in which the shafts rest and which restricts them from rising up or dropping down by holding them to the pad with leather keepers. The pad is prevented from riding forward by a crupper fitted round the horse's tail and attached to the pad by a long back strap.

While the collar and traces are the means by which the horse pulls the vehicle forward, the breeching is fitted to enable the horse to hold the vehicle back. It consists of a broad strap which goes around the horse's backside and is supported by a hip strap which passes over the quarters and through a slot conveniently sewn into the crupper back strap. At each end of the breeching are large brass rings and these are attached to the vehicle shafts by breeching straps. Although this is the most popular form of breeching, there is also another form known as false breeching consisting of a strong strap fixed between the shafts behind the horse. Whereas the first type of breeching can be adjusted so that it is neither too high to slip up under the horse's tail, nor too low to restrict the action of the hind legs, a false breeching can only be used when the height of the vehicle shafts at the back of the horse is correct for his size.

(a)

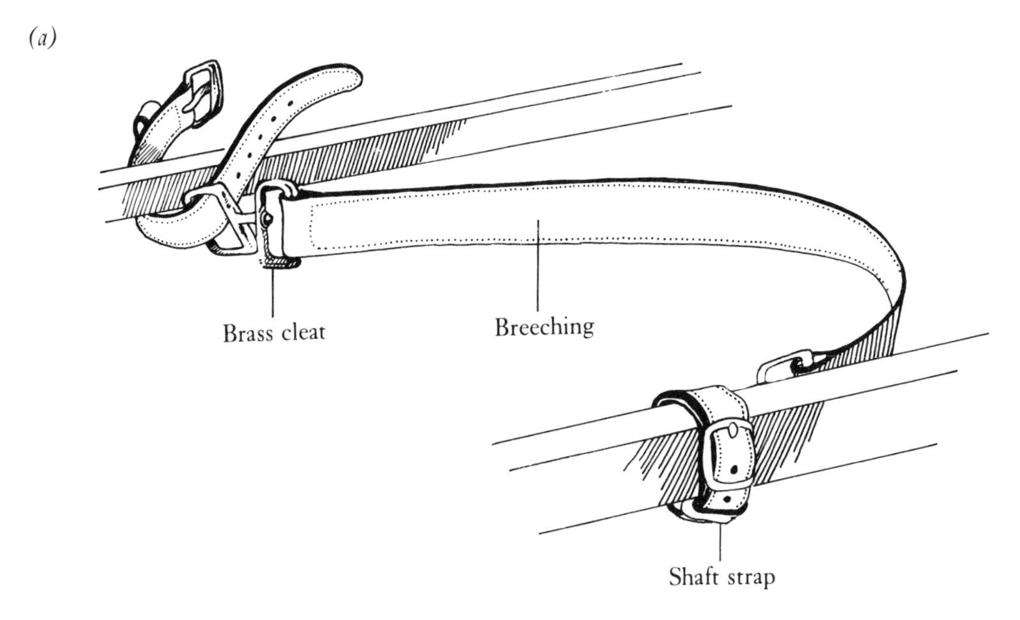

(b)

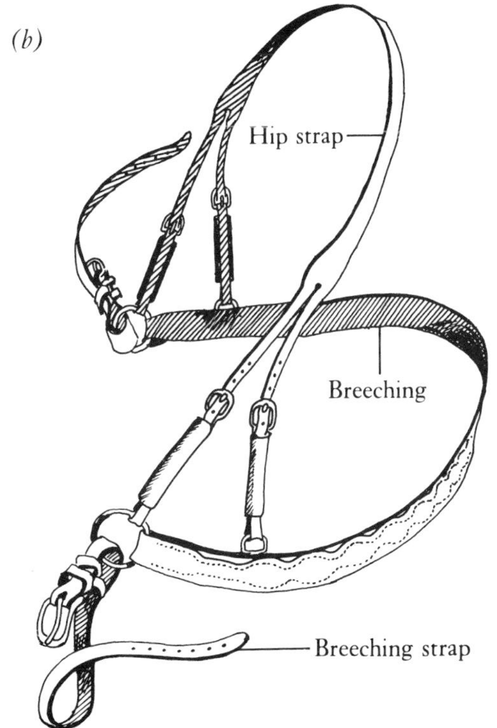

Fig 28 (a) and (b): two types of breeching.

Bridles

The bridle consists of a headpiece which fits over the horse's poll immediately behind the ears. It is held in place by a brow band and these are made in various styles some of which are leather with brass ornamentation and others covered with coloured plastic. At the end of the brow band, where the headpiece straps slide through, there is a brass rosette. Cheek pieces are attached to the headpiece at one end and to the bit at the other and usually incorporate blinkers. These should be adjusted so that the horse's eye is in the centre of the cup. The strap from the centre of the headpiece which connects the blinkers together should be long enough to prevent the blinkers from rubbing on the eyebrow. At the lower end, the cheek pieces pass through the noseband (which should be tighter than a riding noseband to hold them firmly in place) and should then support the bit in the horse's mouth. The noseband should buckle up on the near side with the spare end just long enough to be held neatly in a keeper under the horse's jaw. Some nosebands are made with a separate piece under the jaw which buckles on to either side of the noseband, but having two buckles simply gives you extra to clean. If the horse is in the habit of trying to evade the bit, and continually holds his mouth open, it is possible to use the driving equivalent of a drop noseband which is referred to as a 'flash'. This is a strap, the centre of which is attached by a loop to the centre of the noseband. The strap then passes around the horse's mouth, under the bar of the bit, and fastens behind the horse's jaw.

The whole bridle is secured by a strap passing under the horse's throat and called, for obvious reasons, a throat lash (*see Fig 29*). Reins are traditionally made from leather, long lengths of single thickness being sewn together to give the requisite length. At each end there is a 'billet' or strap, and a buckle with which to attach the reins to the bit.

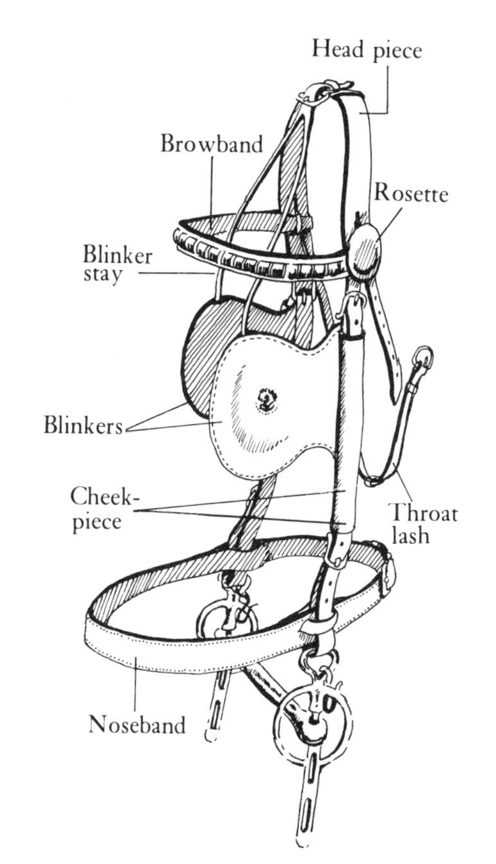

Fig 29 Bridle.

Bits

The key to every horse is to be found in his mouth and that means the selection of the correct bit. In the nineteenth century there was a great variety, as many people had bits forged and ornamented to their own particular preferences. Today these bits have largely been discarded in favour of about half a dozen which are popularly used for driving.

Liverpool (Fig 31)

The Liverpool bit is the most widely used driving bit, usually with a straight bar mouthpiece which is smooth on one side and grooved, or 'rough', on the other, so that it can be reversed according to the softness, or otherwise, of the horse's mouth. It is worn with a curb chain and has four positions in which the reins can be attached. These are:

1. The 'cheek', when the rein is simply buckled to the ring of the bit.
2. The 'rough cheek', when the billet passes round the upright bar while it is still in the ring.
3. The 'middle bar', which is the upper of the two rein slots.

Fig 30 HRH Prince Michael of Kent driving a pair – the nearside horse with a Liverpool bit and off side horse with a snaffle.

Fig 31 Liverpool bit.

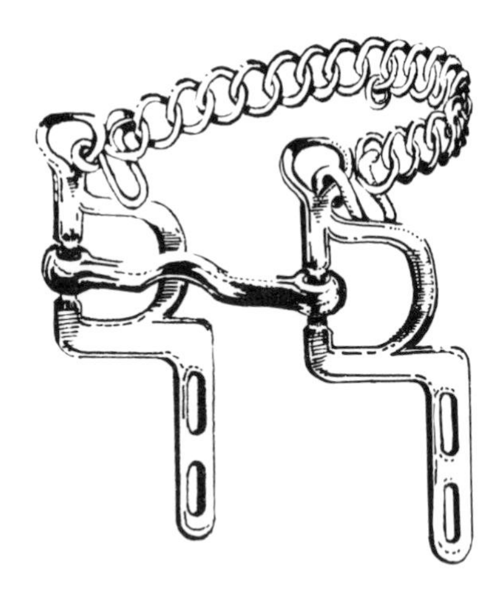

Fig 32 Universal Port-mouth Reversible bit.

4. The 'bottom bar', which is the lowest slot, and the last resort.

The bit should be fitted in the horse's mouth so that the bar of the bit is just wrinkling the corner of his mouth, but only slightly, as a too-tight bit will not be in the correct position on the bars of the mouth. The curb chain should be twisted so that it lies flat in the curb groove, which is just above the horse's lower lip. It should be possible to insert two fingers between the curb chain and jaw when the bit is hanging loose in the horse's mouth.

Universal Port-mouth Reversible Bit (Fig 32)

This has for many years been the standard bit for use with military 'field' saddlery and is also used by mounted police. Its fairly recent popularity with drivers has stressed even more its 'universal' name tag. It has three rein positions and a small port on the mouthpiece which makes it suitable for use on most horses.

Buxton Bit (Fig 33)

This is most favoured by the coaching fraternity as it has a bar connecting the bottoms of the sides of the bit. This is to prevent the bit becoming entangled in the pole chains or any other part of the harness.

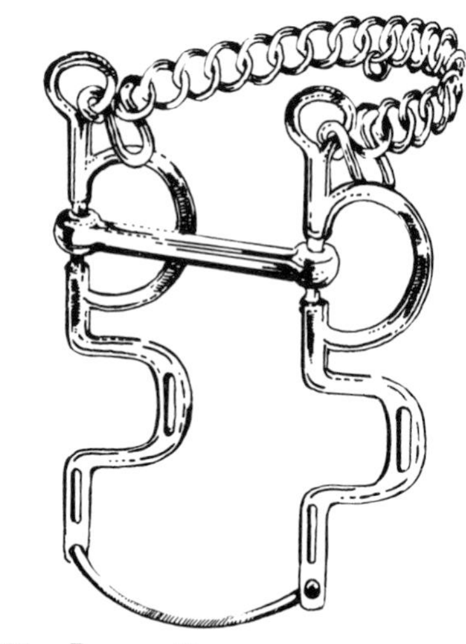

Fig 33 Buxton bit.

Double Ring Snaffle (Fig 34)

This is a very useful bit particularly for schooling horses or when driving on less formal occasions. It is very widely used in Hungary, where it is the usual bit for use with the Hungarian's particular style of breast harness; but it is also very popular with pony drivers as it is well suited to the smaller sets of harness. It can be used with either a plain or twisted mouthpiece and there are several different ways in which the reins can be attached. The snaffle is attached to the cheek pieces by the inner, or 'loose' rings, while the reins can either be attached to both rings together or simply to the outside rings. The latter option will have a more severe 'nutcracker' action on the horse's mouth.

Bearing Reins

Most of us, when we were young, read Anna Sewell's book *Black Beauty* and it was conveyed to our youthful minds that bearing reins were evil devices which caused suffering to the horse. Now is the time to dispel such thoughts because, if properly used, the bearing rein can be a major aid to driving and help to give the horse a correct and balanced head carriage. They can either be attached to the driving bit or, as is most usual, used with a separate bridoon bit. The bearing rein runs from each side of the bridoon bit, through metal loops on the throat lash, and is finally looped over the hook in the centre of the saddle or pad. The foremost part of the rein, which runs through the throat lash ring, is usually of rolled leather which is sewn around a cord to give it added strength.

In single harness the bearing rein is seldom used except for Hackneys, but in double or team harness when the driver is having to cope with the position of more than one horse's head, bearing reins can often be very useful.

Fig 34 Double ring or Wilson snaffle.

Harnessing Up

Horses are very much creatures of habit and get used to things being done in a routine fashion: being fed at a certain time, having their stalls cleaned and being groomed all in a set pattern. They also become easily accustomed to having their harness put on and, again, this should be done in a set order.

The first thing to put on is the collar. The coachmen of old were very superstitious on this point and considered it bad luck if any other piece of harness was put on before the collar. In point of fact, it is most practical to put the collar on first so that the cold leather has a chance to warm to the horse's shoulder before you ask him to pull into it. Put the collar over the horse's head upside down, that is, with the widest part to the top, so that it slips easily over his eyes. If it will not do so, do not attempt to force it but take it

Fig 35 The author driving a team at the Royal Windsor Horse Show, 1969, showing the correct use of bearing reins.

off and stretch it by putting your knee into it and pulling it open. Once it is on, leave it upside-down while you fit the hames to it and buckle them on securely. With the collar just behind the horse's ears, at the narrowest part of his neck, you can now turn it the right way up by rotating it in the same direction as his mane lies. If the horse has a thick neck you can make this operation easier by putting your hand under his jaw and lifting his head slightly. Once the collar is turned, lift it backwards on to his shoulder to avoid dragging it all the way down the mane which you will have spent so much time trimming.

Next the saddle and breeching, all together, are placed on the horse's back. This should be done so that the saddle is slightly behind its intended position and the crupper is lying at the top of the tail. While standing alongside the horse, and not behind him, take the crupper in the right hand and lift it up so that you can put your left hand through it. Run your left hand over the horse's quarters and down his tail until you come to the end of the bony part. Lift the tail gently but firmly and, at the same time with the right hand, slide the crupper over the doubled up tail and place it in the correct position around the base of the tail. Lower the tail with the left hand and then run a forefinger around the inside of the crupper to free any small hairs that may be trapped and could cause the horse discomfort. Now the saddle can be lifted forward into its correct place and the back strap adjusted to ensure that the crupper is held firmly in place. Buckle the girth up tightly, but only do the back band up loosely as this will be adjusted when the horse is in the vehicle. The reins may be put on before the bridle but if the horse is left for a time to warm to his collar you must ensure that the reins are firmly looped up, away from damaging hooves.

A driving bridle is put on in much the same way as a riding bridle. Holding the headpiece in the right hand, by an overhand grip, lay the bit in the palm of the left hand with the thumb over the mouthpiece. In this way the bit can be put into the horse's mouth with the left hand while the right hand pulls the bridle on to the horse's head. The noseband and throat lash can then be done up to secure the bridle properly.

'Putting to' a Single

The term 'putting to' is used for attaching the horse to the vehicle. Before doing so, you should check that all the harness is correctly put on and that the vehicle too is properly prepared, with its cushions and rugs. Safety must always be your prime consideration in everything that you do with horses and carriage, and for this reason you should never go driving without a competent groom to help you. When 'putting to', the groom should position the horse a short distance in front of the vehicle and stand in front of him to prevent him from moving forward. Picking up the shafts you should then draw the vehicle up to the horse, keeping the points of the shafts well above his back until they are far enough forward to be in the right place to slide into the tugs when they are lowered. As you guide one shaft into the tug, your groom can reach forward on the other side of the horse and slip the other tug over the shaft. They should be slid through until the tug is resting against the tug stop on the shaft.

With your groom still standing in front of the horse you should then connect the traces to the vehicle, ensuring that they just pull the collar on to the horse's shoulder while the tug remains correctly positioned in the centre of the saddle skirt. Next you should fasten the breeching strap around the shaft, passing it through the breeching dee on the outside of the shaft. It is also advisable to put the breeching strap around the trace as well, to act as a trace bearer, but this should not be done if it interferes with the line of draught (the straight line which the trace should make from the point at which it attaches to the collar to the trace hook on the vehicle).

Once the horse is attached to the vehicle he should never be left unattended and any harness adjustments should be done carefully and with due regard for safety. *The bridle must never be removed while the horse is attached to the vehicle.* Unless horses are trained to be driven in open bridles, as the Royal Horse Artillery gun teams are, they will take fright on seeing a vehicle tied on behind them. Not only that, but when you remove the bridle you also take the bit out of the horse's mouth and so have no control.

Webbing Harness

As carriage builders have now turned to modern materials and designs to cope with the stress of cross-country driving as it is practised today, so the harness makers have looked for a light, durable and maintenance-free substitute for the traditional leather harness. Most of the manufacturers have turned to some kind of webbing as the basis for their harness. A natural fibre webbing was found to be preferable to nylon webbing as it was less likely to fray, although some traces are still made with a nylon mixture. Washable leather is still used for breast collar lining, breeching lining and pad tops, all parts which press on the horse. The webbing straps provide the strength while the leather provides the comfort. The big advantage of this type of harness is that it is simple to clean. After the mud is removed with a stiff brush, the whole harness can be washed in a bucket of lukewarm water and soap (not detergent).

Tandem Harness

If you want to progress from driving a single horse or pony, the cheapest step is to drive two horses in tandem, but it is by

Fig 36 Mrs Sue Jackson driving a pony in webbing harness.

Fig 37 Tommy Fawcett driving a tandem, showing full collar on the wheeler and breast collar on the leader.

no means the easiest. The lead horse is connected solely by the traces and reins and is free to move in any direction, so he should be very obedient and reliable. The shaft horse in the tandem wears a set of single harness with a few minor alterations. The pad terrets have a roller bar across the centre of them so that the leader rein is separated from that of the shaft horse; the bridle has a Roger ring on the brass rosette, again to carry the leader rein; and the tug buckle has an eye protruding from the lower side, on to which the leader's traces may be clipped (*see Fig 38*). It is also preferable for the shaft horse to have a bit with a bar across the bottom to prevent the leader's reins from becoming entangled with it.

The leader wears a normal bridle and collar (full collar or breast collar is equally acceptable) and a saddle similar to the shaft horse except that it has no back band or slot under the seat. Instead it has two leather strips, sewn to the panel, through which the traces pass. A loin strap and

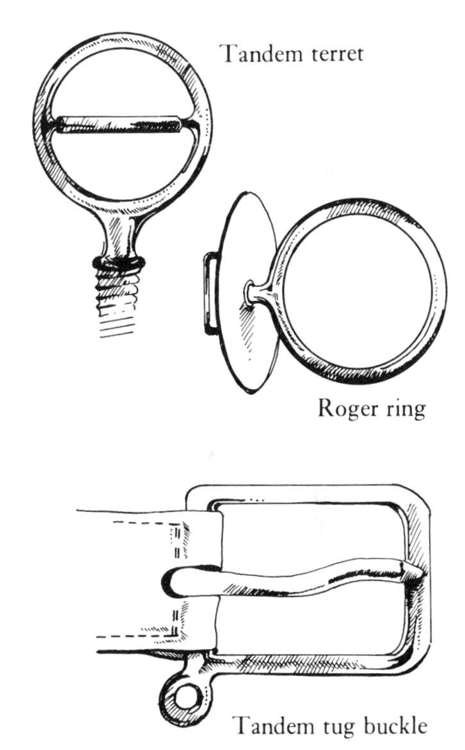

Fig 38 Tandem terret, Roger ring and wheeler tug buckle.

trace bearers are fitted to the crupper back strap. These lie across the horse's hips and hold the traces up to prevent the leader's hind legs or the shaft horse's forelegs becoming entangled with them. There are two types of leader trace. The longer trace has a spring cockeye that clips upwards into the eye of the tug buckle, but ordinary length traces with slot ends can be used in conjunction with a set of leader bars. These two lightweight bars are connected to the shaft horse's collar by a short chain to the kidney link, and two straps with spring cockeyes to the tug buckles *(see Fig 39)*.

Pair Harness *(Fig 40)*

Whereas the rule for single harness is that the straps should all buckle on the near side, with pair harness the rule is that all straps should be buckled on the horse's outside, that is, on the near side of the near side horse and on the off side of the off side horse.

Bridles

The bridles used are similar to those for single harness, with the noseband buckled on the outside of the horse. Every horse is an individual as far as bitting goes but it does look better if the bits on the pair bridles match. In extreme cases it is possible to have different mouthpieces for bits with matching side bars, for example, a Liverpool bit with a straight bar and another one with a port, or half moon curve, in the middle of the bar.

Collars

For a pair it is preferable to use neck collars with hames, which are joined at the bottom with kidney links. Some of these are made in one piece but the most preferable are those that are open or jointed where the links rest against the collar. This enables you to fit the same pair of hames to a different size collar by the simple expedient of using a larger or smaller kidney link. On the bottom of the

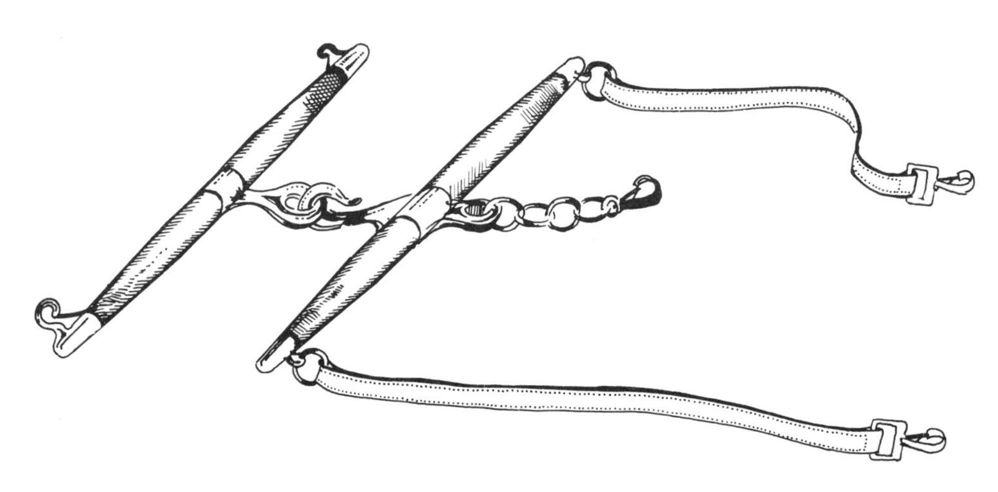

Fig 39 Tandem bars.

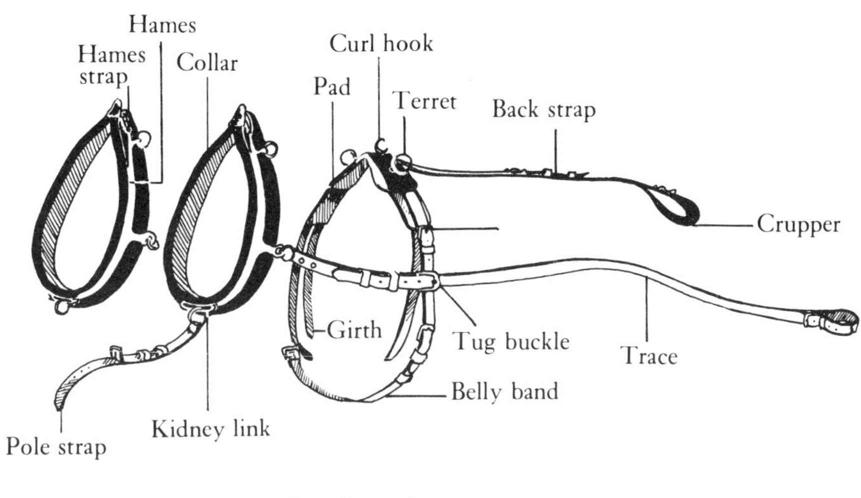

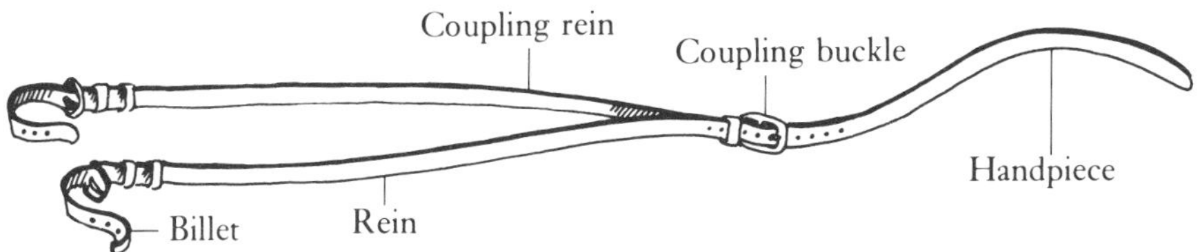

Fig 40 Pair harness.

Fig 41 Greg Willett with his pair of cobs in full collar harness.

Fig 42 Paul Gregory with a pair showing kidney links and breastplates.

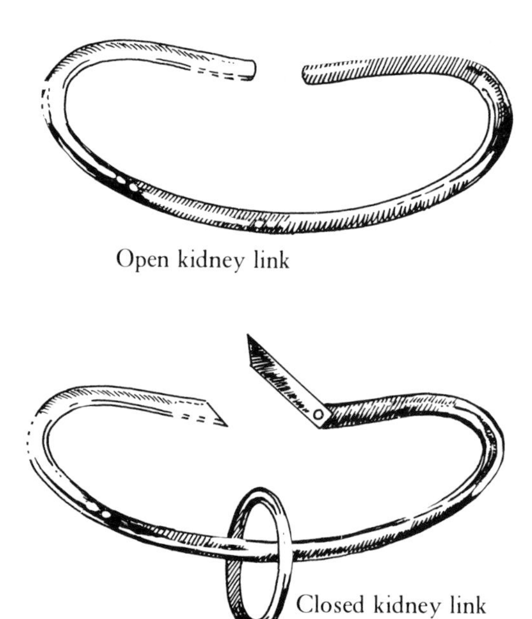

Fig 43 Kidney links, open and closed types.

kidney link there is a loose ring on to which the pole strap or pole chain is attached (*see Fig 43*). The hames' straps at the top of the collars must be buckled from the outside, with the spare end pointing inwards.

If breast collars are used for a pair, it is important that they also have a neck strap. This is a strap that goes through the ring on the centre of the breast collar, round the horse's neck, through a loop on the neck piece of the breast collar, and then buckles on the outside with the spare end of the strap pointing downwards. The purpose of this strap is to assist the horse to pull backwards on the pole head and it should be worn even if breeching is used.

Fig 44 Mrs Jill Holah with a pair of ponies in breast collar harness with correctly fitted neck straps.

Breastplates

These essential items of pair harness also help the horse when he is holding the carriage back. They consist of a strong strap which buckles around the collar and through the kidney link and then passes between the horse's forelegs where it is looped on to the girth. It should not be so short that it pulls the collar down on the horse's neck, but neither should it be so long that it allows the collar to ride up and hit the horse under the chin. If correctly adjusted you should be able to get a hand's width between the breastplate and the horse's chest. Often breastplates have a patent leather front with ornamentation to match the rest of the harness.

Pads

In pair harness the pad is not as important as the saddle in single harness, as it does not have to support the weight of the vehicle. It is, therefore, lighter in construction but it is also made with a metal plate to give it solidity, and with plenty of padding to keep it off the horse's back. On the centre is screwed a curl hook, on to which the bearing rein can be attached, and on either side of this is a rein terret. From each side of the pad comes a strap to support the tug buckles which, for obvious reasons, is known as a tug bearer strap. The girth is made in two pieces, a long piece with a buckle on it and a shorter length which finishes in a strap. These are attached to the pad top with the long length on the inside so that the pad can be fastened from the outside of the horse. A back strap attaches to the dee at the rear of the pad and this strap holds the crupper in place. If trace bearers are used, the loin strap that supports them passes through a loop in the back strap so that it is straight across the horse's hips.

Traces

While these buckle on to the collar at one end, the connection at the vehicle end can take different forms. It is most usual to use one of the three following ends if the vehicle has roller bolts or round-ended swingletrees:

1. The quick release end – probably the most useful, it has a brass runner which goes through a brass slot sewn to the end of the trace (*see Fig 45*). A long leather tongue sewn to the outside of the trace then goes through this runner. This tongue can be quickly pulled out in an emergency and the trace will then come undone. When fitting quick release traces, the long tongue should always face the outside of the horse to whom they are attached so that they can both be easily undone.
2. A similar end, but without the quick release facility, is the running loop (*see Fig 46*). This consists of a brass square which is sewn to the end of the trace, and is then passed back through it to form a running loop, which pulls tight on to the vehicle roller bolt or swingletree. The other side of the brass square usually has a small tongue sewn on to it to enable you to free the loop from the vehicle more easily. As with the quick release end, these tongues should both face outwards when in use.

There is a way of adapting this running loop from traces that have only a slot in the end and this is done by using a metal square with a short T-shaped piece forged or welded on to it. It also has a tongue to assist in easy removal and its application can be seen in *Fig 47*.

3. The last popular trace end for pairs is the French loop (*see Fig 48*), in which the

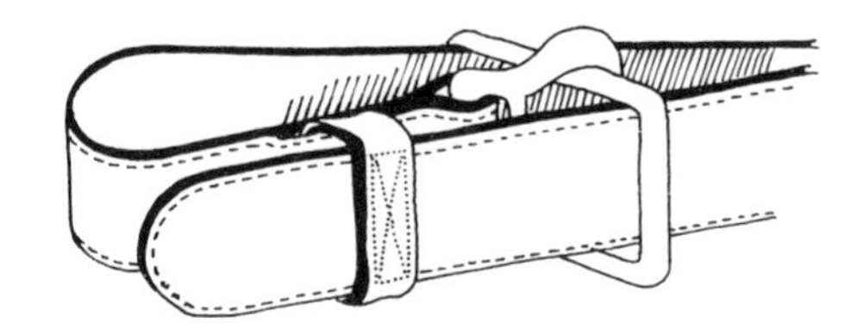

Fig 45 Quick-release trace.

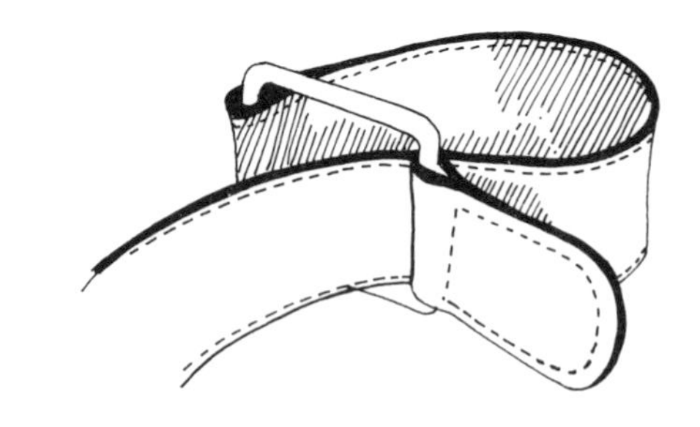

Fig 46 Running loop trace end.

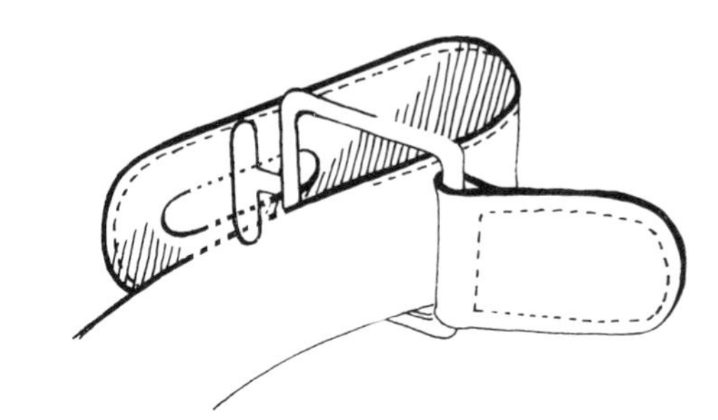

Fig 47 'T' adaptor.

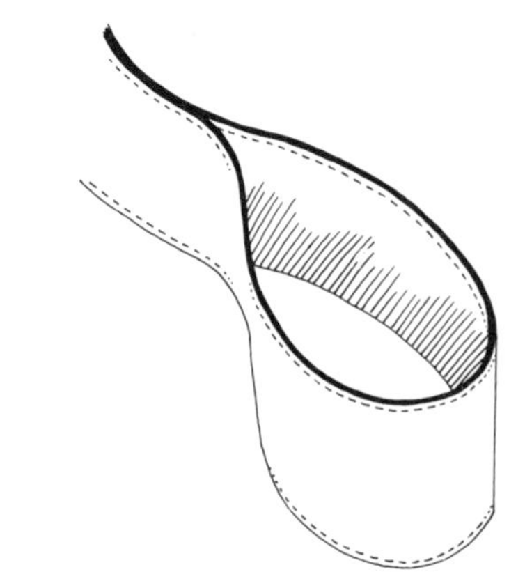

Fig 48 French loop trace.

end of the trace is simply sewn into a loop large enough to go over the roller bolts. This type of end is very popular with drivers of road coaches which have big roller bolts for the trace to fit over, and in days of yore it was particularly useful when teams of horses had to be changed quickly in order not to delay the coach's schedule.

Breeching

This is not always used with a pair but can perform a useful service, particularly with a breast collar. As there are no shafts on to which it can be attached, a different system must be employed. The head of the pole is the part of the carriage by which a pair of horses can hold it back and in a neck collar the well-trained horse will simply hold his head up sufficiently to take the weight on the back of his neck. He can also do this in a breast collar if it is assisted by a neck strap but the breeching makes his task more comfortable. It fits around the horse's backside in the same way as the single breeching, but instead of having straps attaching it to the breeching dees on the shafts it has two long tongues, the same width as the traces, which go into the tug buckles behind the traces. Any forward movement of the carriage can therefore be arrested by the pole straps, collar and breeching which are all connected.

Pole Pieces

Pole straps can vary in kinds, and chains may also be used as pole pieces. These are fastened to the head of the pole and then on to the bottom of the horse's collar by the ring which runs on the kidney link, or to a similar ring attached to a breast collar. Straps can either be plain or of the quick release variety, using a similar system to the quick release traces. Chains also come in two types: those used for light carriage work usually have a spring clip on each end, whereas those used for heavier carriages and coaches have a ring at one end and an open hook at the other. When in use a strong rubber band is usually wound around the hook to prevent it from shaking off the link through which it is placed.

Reins

At first sight, pair reins often baffle a lot of people, but if looked at logically they soon become easy to sort out. Basically, you have two reins and these run from the driver's hands to the outside of each horse. Approximately half-way down each rein, another rein is buckled on, which goes across to the other horse and is called a 'coupling rein'. There are usually plenty of holes where the coupling rein is buckled on to the main rein and these allow for plenty of adjustment when getting a pair of horses balanced to work together. To restrain one horse, you move the coupling buckle on his rein forward and at the same time move the other coupling buckle back by the same number of holes. Most pair reins have a small buckle on one of the driver's hand pieces, and a tongue on the other, so that they can be buckled together when hung in the harness room. This also helps to ensure that you get the correct rein on the right horse. The rein with the buckle should be on the off side horse so that if the rein is thrown over from the near side, when hooking in, it does not have a buckle on it which might hit the driver in the eye.

Fig 49 Paul Tointon at Sandringham in 1983, showing coupling reins crossing from one horse's collar to his partner's bit.

Harnessing a Pair

It is sensible and proper to put the collar on first, as with single harness, and then buckle the hames on in the same way, remembering to ensure that the hames strap points inwards when the collar is correctly positioned on the horse's shoulders. After putting on the breastplate, the pad and crupper are put on next, with the girth of the pad passing through the loop on the end of the breastplate. The traces are then attached to the tug buckles and laid across the horse's back immediately behind the pad. The belly band is then done up, again passing through the loop of the breastplate, and should be tight enough to allow the tug buckle to come away from the horse's sides by about four inches (10cm).

To put the reins on, stand on the outside of the horse and hold the coupling buckle in the right hand. Keeping the rein itself facing towards you, run the left hand down the reins until you come to the bit buckles. Now run the reins through their respective terrets on the pad and collar (that is, the coupling rein through the inside collar and pad terrets, and the outside rein through the outside collar and pad terrets) and then loop the hand piece of the reins through the outside pad terret, securing it around the bearing rein hook. Lastly make a final check that the rein is on the outside of the horse and the coupling rein is on the inside.

The bridle is then put on in the usual way and the outside rein is buckled to the outside of the bit, leaving the coupling rein looped through the collar terret. If the horses are to be led any distance before being put to the vehicle, it is advisable to buckle the coupling rein loosely to the back of the noseband where it cannot fall down and will be handy when the time comes to buckle it to the other horse's bit.

'Putting to' a Pair

The horses should be led up alongside the pole of the vehicle until they are standing in approximately the right place. The groom should then stand in front of them and hold each horse's head by the outside of his bridle where the cheek pieces pass through the noseband. The pole pieces are then loosely attached to the front of the collar and the traces are hooked on to the vehicle. Bearing in mind that everything must be done as safely as possible, the outside trace should always be put on first, followed by the inside trace. If the inside trace is attached before the outside one, and the horse moves, he will be able to swing away from the pole and might take fright on finding the pull on his collar coming from an unusual angle.

The same principle applies when taking the pair out of the vehicle, when the inside trace must be undone and placed over the horse's back before the outside one is detached. Once both traces are hooked on, the pole pieces can be tightened until they are short enough to prevent the horses banging their hocks on the carriage when asked to hold it back.

The coupling reins can now be done up. The horse who holds his head highest should have his coupling rein on the top so that the movement of his head does not interfere with his partner's mouth. Some people think that if the horse with the highest head carriage has his coupling rein underneath, it will help to hold his head down; this is true to an extent but it is done at the expense of a smooth drive.

Team Harness

To progress from a pair to a team requires the addition of two lead horses and some changes to the harness of the two horses alongside the pole, who are now referred to as the wheelers.

Pads

On the leaders, the pads are the same as those used for pair harness, but those used for the wheelers have an added rein terret positioned over the bearing hook on the centre of the pad. Through this terret the leader rein will run back to the driver's hand.

Bridles

The wheeler bridles also have an extra ring fixed to them to accommodate the leader rein. This ring is usually fixed to the brass rosette on the end of the brow band, but can also be hung on a leather strap attached to the head piece or top of the throat lash. The advantage of this latter method is that it allows the wheelers' heads greater freedom of movement, which is especially important when trying to navigate twisty hazards that

Fig 50 HRH The Duke of Edinburgh at Windsor in 1987 driving a team of Fell ponies in open bridles.

require a great deal of articulation between leaders and wheelers.

Collars

While for showing, or coaching, all horses in the team should wear full collars, it is quite permissible to use breast collars on the leaders, or on all four horses for cross-country driving.

Hames

While it is strictly correct for the wheeler hames to have rings on the kidney links, it can also be an advantage to have them on the leader hames so that a connecting strap can be put between the two collars. It also means that a leader can be readily substituted for a wheeler in an emergency. As always, all the hames straps should point inwards.

Breeching and Trace Bearers

While these are not used in the traditional coaching harness, they are both advisable for competition carriage driving. The breeching on the wheelers is the same as that described for use with a pair; and the trace bearers used for the leaders consist of a hip strap passing through the crupper back strap, with a loop buckled on each end. The length of the trace bearer should be such that when the leaders are in draught, the traces ride smoothly through the loops.

Reins

While the wheeler reins are the same as those used for pair driving, the leader reins are necessarily longer. They also have coupling reins used in the same manner and of the same length as those attached to the wheeler reins. When putting the reins on in the stable, they should be folded in half and the loop thus formed should be drawn through the pad terret and collar terret and loosely knotted to the throat lash. This will keep the reins tidily out of the way of the horse's feet as he is led out of the stable to be put to.

'Putting to' the Team

The wheelers are put to first, in the same manner as you would a pair. A groom should then stand to the off side of the wheelers' heads so that he can hold them while the leaders are attached. The leaders are then led into position and stood in their places, a correct distance from the swingletrees to which they will finally be attached. With a groom standing in front of them, the coupling reins are done up and then the reins are run back through the rings on the wheeler bridles, and terrets on the wheelers pads. The near side rein is thrown over to the off side, where all four reins can now be gathered together. Only now should the leader traces be hooked on to the swingletrees, so that, should there be any trouble, the coachman has all the reins together and can quickly pick them up to assume control. The outside traces should again be attached to the swingletrees first, and the inside ones are the very last item on the team to be attached. Before getting on to the vehicle, the driver should walk round the team and check that everything is correct and ready to drive.

On completion of the drive, the horses should be taken out of the vehicle by the same procedure in reverse. While the driver is still holding the reins, the grooms should undo the leader traces, inside ones first, and lay them tidily over the horse's back. They then pull the leader reins from the driver's hands and loop them through the terrets. The coupling reins should now be undone and one groom remains at the leaders' heads while the other groom uncouples the wheelers, helped by the driver who has now got down from the vehicle. Once the team are completely disconnected they are led off together to the stables.

4 Vehicles

It is always difficult to decide which comes first, the horse or the carriage. Some people will buy a particular type of horse to suit the carriage that they already own, while others will look for a carriage to suit a favourite horse. These are only two considerations to be reviewed when contemplating the acquisition of a carriage. Another salient factor is what exactly you want the vehicle for, and, last, but by no means least, how much you can afford to spend.

The use to which the vehicle is to be put is really the most important consideration; it can either be for showing or for competitive driving, by which is meant the rugged cross country. For showing, the older, original vehicles are obviously preferred, while for competing there is a new breed of custom-built carriages.

Traditional Vehicles for Showing

Single Pony

The most popular sector in showing is the single pony class, for many reasons, some of which have already been discussed. As there are many excellent ponies it becomes even more important to find a vehicle to complement the animal that you intend to show. Bearing in mind your own size, you should look for a vehicle that will suit both you and your pony for size and comfort. Although it is not necessary to have your groom riding with you when in the show ring, you should ensure that there will be room for a groom in the carriage so that you can also enter competitions that entail a drive out of the arena.

As most ponies for showing have an air of daintiness about them – some rather more than others – the ideal vehicle should complement this quality. Of the traditional vehicles a suitably-sized stick-back gig fills all these requirements. Alternatively, the ralli car comes in a range of sizes, some of which are suitable for ponies. This type of vehicle was built in very large numbers in the early part of this century and was based on the style of the dogcart. It was designed to be a family vehicle, holding two adults and two children, with space under the seat for a picnic hamper. The panel sides curved upwards to finish in a mudguard over the wheels, which meant that no part of the wheels could be reached from inside the vehicle by inquisitive young arms. This made it safe for the carriage of very young children.

Another pony vehicle that was similarly safe for children was the governess cart, many of which survive to this day and are still to be seen in showing classes. Originally built in large quantities for governesses to take their charges out for a drive, they incorporated several safety factors. For instance, the tub-shaped body was usually hung on elliptical springs within a cranked axle which gave the vehicle a very low centre of gravity and therefore made it difficult to turn

Fig 51 Mr P. Froggatt driving his Welsh cross bay gelding pony to a stick back gig.

over. The one door by which everyone got into the vehicle was situated at the rear and had the handle on the outside only, where it could be reached by the driver when seated in the right rear corner. One of the main drawbacks was that it was necessary to sit at an angle when driving which can become uncomfortable over long periods. It was also difficult to get out of the vehicle quickly and to reach the pony's head should the need arise.

While most ponies are driven to two-wheeled vehicles, there is a four-wheeled pony phaeton which is quite popular, although not many are still in use. Again, this was usually driven by an adult when taking children out for a drive or picnic and several elegant examples may still be seen in carriage collections at various places around the world.

Single Horse

For the single horse there is a much greater range of vehicles available, as more of these seem to have survived the depressed years of carriage driving in the thirties and forties. They fall largely into two main categories – gigs and dogcarts – although within these two types are a multitude of variations, as different coach builders and designers produced their own vehicles. Gigs were the original two-wheeled vehicle and were designed to carry just two people facing forward. Early models were simply suspended on leather braces inside a wooden framework to which the wheels were attached, but with the invention of the elliptical spring they became much more sophisticated and comfortable.

Tilbury was a very popular coach builder and built a gig to the design of The Hon. Fitzroy Stanhope. This incorporated his own springing system – two transverse springs and two semi-elliptical springs – which gave an extremely comfortable ride to the vehicle's occupants, particularly over rough country roads. These Stanhope gigs were extremely popular and were made in such large quantities that quite a few excellent examples survive today. Another builder who used a similar springing system, but with only one transverse spring instead of two, was Mr Bennett. Somehow his name got misspelt and the gig was known as the Dennett gig – another popular member of the large family of two-wheeled vehicles.

The other branch of the family is the very popular dogcart. It was so named because the sporting gentleman would use it to convey his dogs with him when out for a day's shooting or coursing. Because of this, it usually had louvres or slatted sides so that the dogs could breathe more easily and there was some ventilation for the wet, smelly creatures after a day's sport. The seat was moveable and could accommodate two people

Fig 52 Mr F. Todd driving his grey mare to a C-spring dogcart.

facing forward and two facing backwards. The tail-board was hinged at the bottom and let down to become a footboard for those on the rear seat. It was a versatile vehicle and many uses were found for it apart from its primary sporting role. With its drop-down tail-board it was also useful for the conveyance of luggage to and from the railway station, or purchases from the local store. It was the most popular vehicle in country areas and bred different versions, many of which took their names from the area in which they were used – Essex, Norfolk, Stratford and Whitechapel, for example.

Pairs

For tandem driving a higher version of the dogcart was required, in order to give the driver a better view of his lead horse. Because the lead horse could sometimes go astray and require the quick attention of the groom, it was not always satisfactory to have him facing backwards on such a dog cart, so the cocking cart also became popular with tandem drivers in the late nineteenth century. On this vehicle, both seats were facing forward so that the groom could see what was going on and anticipate when his master was going to need assistance.

Larger versions of the dogcart were made with four wheels and could be adapted for use either with a large single horse or fitted with a splinter bar and pole for a pair. Where pairs are shown in the ring these days they are usually driven to either a dogcart, wagonette, or phaeton.

A wagonette was in fact the smaller version of the larger luggage brake and had a seat at the front for the driver and one other, while the back had seats on both sides, facing inwards, and could usually accommodate four people, although there was very little leg room when the vehicle was fully laden.

The name phaeton has been accorded to a large variety of four-wheeled vehicles, the most notable early example being the high-flyer phaeton of the Prince Regent (later George IV) who was himself a very keen whip. From this developed the crane-necked phaeton, so called because of the bent iron frame which allowed the front wheels to turn completely underneath, giving a full lock. This was very useful for turning in narrow places but when the roads became wider in the early nineteenth century the crane-necked phaeton went out of fashion and was replaced by the mail phaeton and the demi-mail phaeton. These were more robust vehicles, the former having a perch and undercarriage similar to a mail coach, while the latter simply had elliptical springs bolted directly on to the body for the rear wheels, with the turntable for the front wheels similarly directly mounted. Many of these have survived until today and are popular in showing classes.

Even more popular, however, is the elegant spider phaeton which was first produced in America and is now widely used there and in Britain for showing pairs of horses. Its light skeletal frame and elegant lines make it the ideal vehicle to show horses to their best advantage. It can be used with a pair of shafts for a single, but is better suited to a pair.

Four-in-hand

The most usual class for showing four-in-hand teams is the coaching class, which is a major feature of many large horse shows. However, not everyone can

Fig 53 John Parker driving his team to a demi-mail phaeton.

Fig 54 Mrs B. Metcalfe driving an early Bennington.

afford the expense of one of these super equipages and it is then that we see one of the largest of the phaeton family. The Beaufort phaeton has a high front seat which makes it ideal for team driving and it was from one of these that Michael Mart took his pattern for the team vehicles that he builds for competition driving. With the introduction of driving competitions, it soon became evident that not only would there not be enough fine, original vehicles to cater for all the new-comers, but it would also be sacrilegious to give these fine antiques the rough usage that would be experienced on the cross-country section of the competition. This led to the modern breed of coach builders who took their ideas from older carriages but reproduced them using modern techniques and materials.

Modern Vehicles for Teams and Pairs

Wheels

Some of the early examples of modern vehicles incorporated quite a lot of wood, but as the severity of the competitions increased, so the wooden parts were, in the main, discarded and replaced with sturdier metal. The wheels were amongst the first things to be changed. The wooden wheels, with their peripheral brakes and protruding hubs, were re-placed with aluminium wheels which looked similar except that they did not have long hubs but were mounted on brake drums similar to those on a car. In some cases disc brakes were used, and these have now largely taken over from

Fig 55 David Brand driving a modern metal phaeton.

drum brakes, although the basic concept of the smooth-hubbed metal wheel has been retained.

In the original carriages, the front wheels were traditionally smaller than the rear wheels. This was necessary to allow room between the axle and floor of the carriage for a turntable, and also to allow the smaller wheels to pass under the carriage when turning. The disadvantage of small wheels on cross country was that they could not surmount obstacles, large stones, etc. with the same ease as a larger wheel, and caused more drag when driving through loose sand or heavy mud. It was, therefore, going to be preferable to have the front wheels the same size as the rear wheels and the builders looked for their inspiration and ideas to the equirotal designs first tried out by W. Bridge Adams in the 1830s. To get round the problem of the wheels turning under the carriage, Adams had moved the pivot from its normal place under the front seat to half-way along the vehicle. This meant that the front half of the carriage was always directly behind the horses, while the rear half articulated separately. The Prestiegne Carriage Company began producing vehicles for cross-country driving which employed this principle, but it was found that these 'bendys', as they were called, could not last long with the extreme pressures which were exerted on the one pivot point. While some of the lighter models are still in use for pairs, the heavier ones built for teams have now been mainly

Fig 56 David Brand driving a modern cross-country vehicle with equal sized wheels.

Fig 57 John Richards driving a Presteigne 'Bendy' at Scone Palace in 1984.

Fig 58 Peter Munt driving a modern Bennington Beaufort phaeton.

discarded as unreliable. While acknowledging the principle of keeping the front wheels as large as possible, carriage designers have now returned to the original concept of a fore-carriage which turns beneath the driver, with an arch in the vehicle body under which the front wheels can turn.

Although not yet internationally accepted, British team carriages are now built with the wheeled track width at 160 centimetres, which is the required width for cone driving, but if the vehicles are also required for use on the cross country they have an adjustment which enables the axles to be shortened to 125 centimetres.

Springing and Suspension

While semi-elliptical springing is still used on modern phaetons, to retain a modicum of similarity to the original vehicles, these springs are now assisted by the use of hydraulic shock absorbers. Such hydraulic assistance is also applied to the latest type of pole suspension. Early poles bounced up and down with the vehicle's fore-carriage, of which they were an integral part, and then progressed to being mounted on a spring at the tail end of the pole where it was fixed to the carriage. Now, with the aid of springs and shock absorbers, the pole floats freely and is not affected by the movement of

Fig 59 Mrs Philippa Gammell driving a 1986 Bennington pony pair vehicle.

the carriage. Another improvement to the pole was the introduction of a dog-leg bend just in front of the fore-carriage, which lessens the chance of a horse getting a hind leg over the pole, or seriously knocking a hock when turning in a tight hazard.

It was obvious that as the sport progressed drivers would become more expert, course builders more ingenious and carriage builders would therefore continue to experiment. In 1986 Dobroslav Kubista of Czechoslovakia tried out an air suspension system which was used by Josef Dymes Senior at the World Championships that year, but it has yet to be proved better than the suspension systems in use at present.

Seating

While it is necessary to have a seat wide enough to accommodate the driver and a referee, the actual style of the driver's seat, or box seat as it is more traditionally known, is a matter for personal preference. Ideally the driver should sit on a sloping cushion which is high enough to enable him to have his legs fairly straight. The footboard on which he stands should be at a comfortable angle so that no undue stress is exerted on the ankles; it should also encourage him to sit up straight when driving. This upright stance also helps him to exert a strong pull on his horses should the need arise. The rails around the box seat should be high enough to prevent the driver from slipping off, but should not interfere with his arm movement or the ability to lean backwards. An interesting box seat rail was devised by the late John Ravenscroft, who angled the rails slightly over the driver's legs, which gave him a greater sense of security while not trapping him on to the carriage.

The rear half of the carriage body, when in use for presentation and dressage, should have a forward-facing seat where the two grooms can observe all that the driver is doing and be available to assist him on request. Access to this seat should be by steps on the rear of the vehicle. Marathon vehicles have an open body at the rear to enable the grooms to get in and out freely and an ample step on which a groom can stand to help swing the vehicle around a tight turn. There are no seats in this open back so the grooms can stand and deploy their weight as the terrain demands.

Modern Vehicles for Singles and Tandems

Wheels

As with the team vehicles, a great deal of experimentation has gone on over the years to arrive at a vehicle which, as well as being worthy of show class presentation, is also suitable for the marathon phase. Wheels were again the first major consideration and were made of metal to give them the strength to endure pounding over rough going. At first they were kept as large as possible, to give a smoother ride, but this also raised the centre of gravity and made the carriage more liable to tip over. To counteract this, a back step was devised that could be bolted on for cross-country driving, on which the groom could stand and greatly reduce the top-heaviness. It also gave the groom greater freedom of movement, so that he could help stabilise the carriage. It did, however, upset the front to rear

Fig 60 A wooden Harewood dogcart being used as a marathon vehicle.

Fig 61 John Ravenscroft in a home-built cross-country vehicle competing in the National Championships in 1982.

balance, which is all-important to the horse's comfort in a two-wheeled vehicle. Even if the driver had a sliding seat it meant that he would have to go so far forward that his knees would be uncomfortably tight to the dashboard, putting him in a position that would make driving for any length of time a strain, and also very unsightly. The solution was found in having a sliding body – while the shafts and wheels remained constant, the body could be moved forward to counterbalance the weight of the groom.

Seating

Having the seat to himself, the driver now tended to slide from side to side and in order to check this, special cushions were devised to hold the driver in place. Another idea was that a separate box seat should be added for marathons which slotted into the existing seat and had its own seat rails to stop the driver from slipping. It was held in place by a strap screwed to the main seat.

As a five-section marathon is a long way for a groom to stand, a 'seat' can also be provided for him in the shape of a strong wooden disc, like the top of a bar stool, with a strong rope through its centre attaching it to the vehicle. By standing astride this rope, the groom can sit on his 'bar stool' seat for the longer stretches of the journey, and when not in use it simply hangs under the back of the vehicle.

Four-wheelers

In recent years experiments have been done with four-wheeled vehicles for singles and tandems, but at the time of

Fig 62 An early single four-wheeled vehicle that did not prove very successful.

writing there have not been any startling results from these. While four wheels are undoubtedly more stable than two, the horse has twice the number of wheels to tow along which, while it may make little difference on tarmac roads or hard, smooth going, is bound to be much more difficult in sand, loose soil, or mud.

As a training aid, a four-wheeler could be very useful, but unless you are extremely affluent it is a luxurious expense on top of everything else that must be afforded if you are to compete.

One vehicle can really be utilised for all phases of the competition. With modern techniques, builders can now make interchangeable shafts and wheels so that a smart set can be retained for presentation and dressage while a more workmanlike set is brought into use for the marathon. Not only is this a cheaper solution than having two carriages, but it greatly cuts down the transport problem when going to events.

5 Breaking and Training

Much has been written on the subject of breaking horses to ride, and their training for the various ridden fields, from show-jumping to *haute école* dressage; it is not my intention to encroach on any of these subjects here, but to describe the methods that should be used in the training and schooling of horses and ponies for driving. Much of this will necessarily be the same as, or will repeat, the training given to a riding horse. Where this happens, however, it will only be because it is essential for what we intend to do, which is to produce a well-trained and properly schooled driving horse. Let us therefore presume at the onset that the horse or pony has already been mouthed and broken to ride, and we are now about to introduce him to the pleasures of carriage driving.

Lungeing

The first essential quality of a driving horse is that he goes forward freely without too much urging, and that he

Fig 63 Peter Munt's well-trained team going on freely at the National Championships in 1986.

does not allow things to distract him unduly. Obviously any horse will shy away from a sudden or frightening movement, but the ideal horse for driving should be steadier than most. He must also work to a greater extent on words of command, for the voice is one of the driver's main aids. To achieve freedom of movement and obedience to the voice it is best to commence training on the lunge. For this you require a lungeing cavesson, which is a form of headcollar with a padded noseband, on the front of which there is a metal plate. On the metal plate there are three swivel rings to which the lunge rein can be attached. It is usual to buckle the long lunge rein to the centre ring, while the two side rings can be used for side reins if you are not lungeing with a bit in the horse's mouth. The cavesson also has a jowl strap which prevents it being pulled into the horse's eyes.

A surcingle or breaking pad should be used in conjunction with the cavesson and to this the side reins can be buckled. If it is a plain surcingle, the side reins can easily be looped on to it and an additional strap passed over the withers between the two reins to prevent them slipping down too far and pulling the horse's head

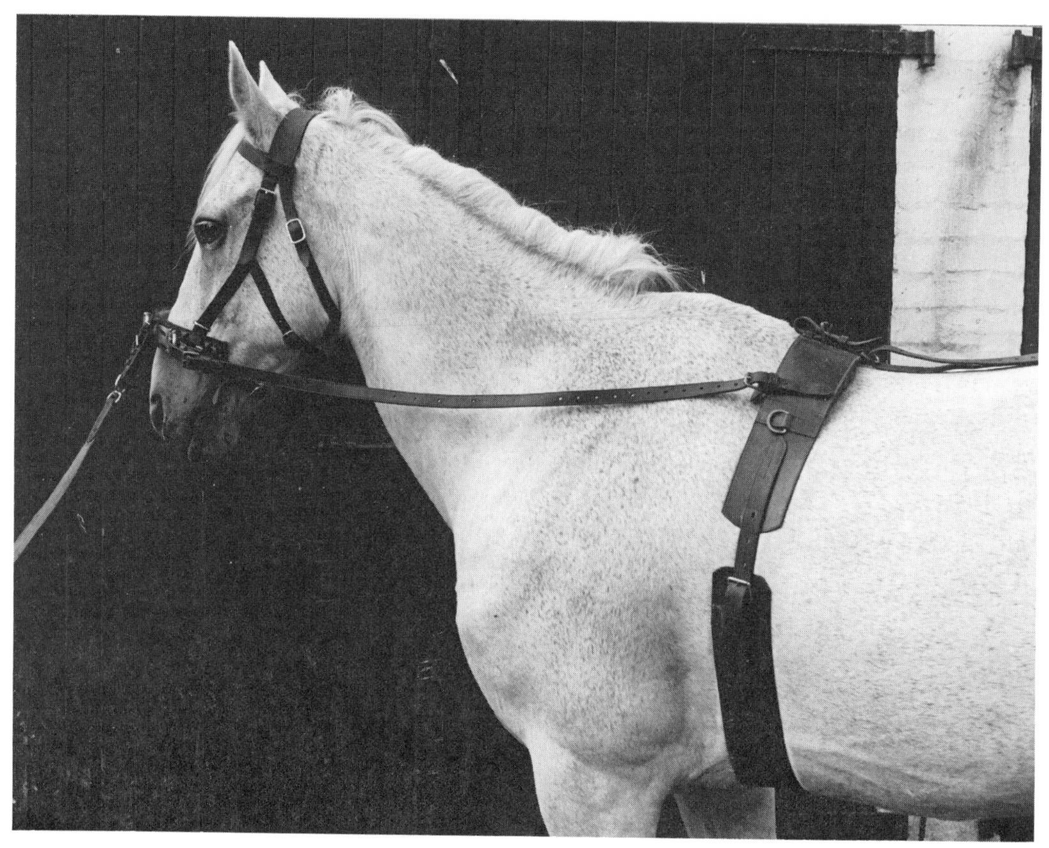

Fig 64   A horse in lungeing cavesson and side reins.

down. The inside rein should always be the tighter, so that the horse's head is slightly bent to the direction in which he is going. This is only a small adjustment because the horse should be lunged in as large a circle as the rein will allow. The relative lengths of these side reins should be altered when changing direction so that the horse is always looking slightly inwards to where you are standing, and never looking away from you.

Stand in the centre, and if the horse is going to the left, hold the lunge rein in your left hand and whip in your right. Ensure that you keep the rein carefully looped in your hand, paying out and drawing it in as required, and not allowing it to trail on the ground where it can quickly become entangled with feet – either yours or the horse's – with disastrous effect. The whip should be held up off the ground, with the end of the lash held against the handle where it can be released if required. You should stand so that you are slightly behind the horse, but well out of kicking range, and the angle between the arm holding the rein and that holding the whip should be approximately 60 degrees. Start the horse walking around you in a small circle at first and gradually pay out the lunge rein until he is going in as big a circle as the rein will allow. Do not follow the horse round, but stand on a central spot and pivot as the horse walks round. If he will not walk on at first, you should get someone to lead him forward until he gets the idea. Do not chase him with the whip, which should only be used to encourage him into a change of pace, or when lagging behind his work.

Verbal Commands

Your words of command should be given in a clear, firm voice – not shouted – taking care to make each one distinctly different. When moving off from the halt it is always best to give a cautionary word so that the horse is prepared for the actual command. For example, I always say 'All right, walk on', with a slight pause after the first word to let it register with the horse before giving the actual command. The word 'walk' should also be drawn out so that it is not confused with the command to stop, which is usually 'whoa', given in a short manner. The command to trot is usually given as a two-syllable word – 'ter-rot' – so that once again it is a different sound and one which the horse will associate with the act of trotting.

Harness Training

Once you have got the horse lungeing properly and changing pace correctly on your word of command, it is time to start thinking about the harness. Having got the harness correctly fitted, you should begin by taking the horse for a led walk wearing his harness, with the exception of the bridle, reins and traces. The breeching straps should be buckled forward on to the collar tug buckles, not tightly, but just so that the horse will get used to the collar against his shoulders and the breeching around his backside. If the area in which you are training is fairly quiet, this exercise could be carried out in a stable headcollar, but otherwise a snaffle bridle should be used.

When he is used to walking in harness, the cavesson can be put on and he can

Fig 65 Horse being lunged in harness.

now be lunged in harness. If the previous lungeing has been well taught then there is no reason why this should not go smoothly.

At this point in his education it is a good idea to introduce the horse to trotting poles. These are simply jumping poles laid on the ground parallel with each other and sufficiently far apart to make the horse trot properly over them. If he tends to have a lazy action these poles can be raised slightly off the ground (possible by putting either end on a house brick) so that he picks up his feet. When using the trotting poles it is best to start with two until you are sure that you have got them the correct distance apart, and when the horse is going easily over these you can increase the number of poles.

Longreining

The next part of the horse's education is to be driven in long reins, wearing his harness as he did when you were lungeing him. It is best to start with an open bridle, but using the bit in which you eventually intend to drive him. A riding bridle can be utilised for this purpose; the long reins should run from the bit, through the collar terrets and pad terrets

Fig 66 Driving in long reins.

before dropping either side of the horse's hind quarters to the driver's hands. It is essential that you have someone to assist you when schooling a young driving horse, and in this instance they should be standing at the horse's head while you run the reins back and position yourself behind the horse. When longreining, it is advisable to hold a rein in each hand, with the lungeing whip carried in the right hand. If required, the thong should be laid along the horse's side so that the tip of it strikes the shoulder between the collar and the pad. Never strike the horse with the stock of the whip and *never* hit him on the rump. As you give the horse the cautionary word, the helper should quietly stand to one side so that the horse can move forward when asked to do so.

If he is at all hesitant, the helper can simply lead him forward for a pace or two and then walk alongside while you are driving him. When you feel that the horse is going forward well, you can tell the helper to drop back and walk alongside you, but be readily available to run to the horse's head should the need arise.

Having got him going forward freely in an open bridle once or twice, you should then put his blinkered driving bridle on and repeat the same routine of longreining. The only difference this time is that, should the helper go to the horse's head, he should approach the horse from such an angle that the horse will be able to see him before he takes hold of his head.

Learning to Pull

Now we come to the serious business of getting the horse to pull, and this step requires at least two helpers. The traces should be buckled on to the tugs before you begin and then laid across the horse's back just behind the pad. The breeching straps should be buckled into loops and left to hang at the horse's side. Long-reining should be commenced in the normal manner the horse has become used to over the past days of his training, with one helper now walking on either side of the horse just behind his pad. When the horse has settled down to his work and is walking freely, the helpers, acting on your instructions should gently lift the traces off the horse's back. Keeping them away from his side, they should slide their hands down them until they are holding each trace about six inches (15cm) from the end. The helper on the left should hold the trace in his right hand and the helper on the right should hold

Fig 67 Learning to pull.

the trace in his left hand. Acting on your instructions (because as well as driving the horse you will be monitoring all his reactions) they should now let the traces gently flap against the horse's side to let him know that they are there. After doing this for a while the traces should be pulled taut so that the collar is just held firmly on to the horse's shoulder.

If the horse resists at any stage of his training, you should go back to the last movement at which he was successful, settle him to that, and then attempt to progress once more. Presuming that he is accepting all that you are now asking him to do, the helpers can take a slightly firmer pull on the traces and the horse should respond with a slight lowering of the head as he pulls into his collar. Having let him pull for a short distance, you should then stop and the helpers should release the pressure as he halts. When you ask him to walk on, the helpers should remain stationary until the horse actually pulls them forward and they can then resume the gentle pulling on the traces. After several stops and starts the horse will realise what he is supposed to be doing and the helpers can exert a greater pull on the traces as the horse warms to his collar.

The next step should be a repeat of this lesson but over gently undulating ground. This time the helpers should hold the trace in one hand and the looped breeching strap in the other, so that as the horse walks uphill they pull on the traces, and as he goes downhill they slacken the traces, holding the breeching tight around his backside. The driver must be particularly wary at this point that he is not too close to the back legs which may come flying out the first time the horse feels the breeching. If he is at all worried by the breeching you must quietly persevere until he accepts it naturally and without the slightest sign of a kick, or even a change of pace. Having got that sorted out you will know the front of your carriage should be fairly safe!

It is a good idea at this stage to get him to drag a dead weight such as a log or large motor tyre. To do this you should run the traces through the looped breeching straps and then attach short lengths of rope to them so that the dead weight is about three feet (90cm) behind the horse. Whilst doing this exercise it is essential to have somebody near his head so that as soon as you stop him they can hold him and prevent him from stepping backwards, which could result in a nasty tangle and a frightened horse.

Before asking him to go between the shafts of your precious carriage, it is a good idea to get two broom handles for your helpers to hold in the tugs and against the horse's side so that he is prepared for the next step. On the day you intend to put him between the shafts, it is preferable to give him some long-reining first so that he settles into his usual routine of being driven. Then, with someone standing in front of him and holding his head, you can bring the carriage up behind him, the shafts being held well up and lowered only when they are level with the tugs and can then be slipped quietly through them. All movements should be done quietly and with the minimum of fuss. Whilst you and one of your helpers hold the shaft in the tug, the person at the horse's head should just lead him forward a few steps and then stop, in order for him to feel and hear the vehicle behind him.

If he seems to accept this quietly enough, you can then gently attach the traces to the carriage, do up the breeching straps and check the tightness of the belly band. Take the reins to the off side of the vehicle and stand alongside so that you will now be able to drive the horse without actually being in the vehicle. Your helper at the horse's head should move away on your command and walk alongside the horse's neck so that his head can be quickly held if required. It is sometimes useful to leave a webbing headcollar on underneath the bridle, to which a clip rope can be attached for the initial leading and then quickly detached when you have got him going.

For this first drive in shafts you should attempt to go in as straight a line as possible, frequently stopping and starting to get him very used to the movement of the carriage behind him. When this has been accomplished, you can now get into the vehicle very quietly and, with someone at his head, ask him to walk on again. Balance the vehicle so that the weight is only just resting on the tugs and the horse should then walk forward freely. Up to this point most of your work on long reins has been done at the walk (unless you are very energetic) so keep driving at the walk until you are completely sure

Fig 68 Edwina Hart driving Timber Falling Parsley at Scone in 1985.

that the horse has accepted the vehicle and is happy in his work. It is not practical to keep driving in a straight line and you will inevitably come to a corner, so to prepare for this you should drive in as large a circle as possible to get the horse used to turning. He will not understand why he cannot bend his body at first, but will soon learn that only his head can turn and he must come round within the confines of the shafts. Having driven in a large circle, you should drive in a large figure-of-eight, very gradually making it smaller so that the horse learns to turn in both directions.

The First Drive

Now you should be ready to go for your first quiet drive. It is always preferable to start out at a walk so that the horse settles down, and this also gives you a chance to check that you have all the harness correctly adjusted. The first trot should be only on your word of command, and before starting again, ensure that the weight of the vehicle is just resting on the tugs. You do not want the vehicle to start bouncing as soon as he trots because this may be unnerving for the horse, as well as uncomfortable for you and your groom.

Fig 69 A well-trained pony standing still after a wheel collapse.

Choose a quiet route for your first drive and one that is not too long. On your return to the stables, in a state of elation that you have successfully trained your horse, give him some reward to thank him for doing so well. When you take his harness off, rub some alum or surgical spirit into his shoulders where the collar has been pressing, in order to alleviate any slight brusing and to harden up his shoulders. This should be done after every outing for the first week, and periodically after that, whenever he has had a particularly hard drive.

Training a Pair

Having trained a single driving horse, it is not so very difficult to persuade him to go in a pair with another horse. It will be strange for him at first so, once again, his conversion should be undertaken in unhurried stages.

It is always best to put a young horse in beside an older 'schoolmaster' who can be relied upon to get on with his job quietly while you are concentrating on the new boy. Once again you need your helpers, at least two, and should begin by long-reining the two horses as a pair. While they are standing together with someone at their heads, link their two collars together with a strap or rope attached to the kidney link rings and then couple their heads together with the reins. After positioning yourself behind them, get your helpers to lead them forward by the outside of their bridles on your word of command. You should then be able to assume control as they go forward without being led, and your two helpers can just hold the outside trace of each horse to check any tendency to swing outwards. Having got them used to going together, you can put them into the vehicle.

Hook the schoolmaster in first and check that he is correctly poled up so that he can move off once the young horse is beside him. Now stand the young one alongside the pole and loosely attach the pole strap. It is preferable that you use quick release pole straps and traces at this point, just in case things do not go well and you need to release the horse in a hurry. Attach the outside trace first and then quietly lean over and attach the inside one. Couple their heads with the reins and gradually tighten the young horse's pole strap to the correct length.

Mount the carriage and take up your reins so that you have gentle contact on both their mouths. Make sure that your schoolmaster is standing well up into his collar so that when you ask them to walk on he will set the vehicle in motion. Have your whip ready so that you can quietly encourage the young horse if he shows any reluctance to go forward. Now adopt the same driving techniques as you did with the single horse – straight line, large circle and figure-of-eight until the young horse is accustomed to the fact that he has a pole on only one side, and not so close to him as were the shafts. Although it is best to keep the horse on the same side during his training, he should occasionally be changed over during schooling to prevent him from becoming bored or lop-sided in his pulling.

Tandem Driving

It is cheaper to progress from singles to tandems than it is to pairs because with a tandem you can usually use the same vehicle that you had for your single and it

Fig 70 Louise Serjeant with her mother as groom in a vehicle built by her father.

Fig 71 Graeme Whittaker showing that tandem driving has its problems.

Fig 72 George Bowman's Lippizaners bowing to Her Majesty The Queen at Sandringham Driving Trials.

is only the harness that is the additional expense. A tandem is more difficult to drive than a pair because you have two more reins to hold in your hand, but the schooling is easier because having a leader in front of your single horse is basically only an extension of the long rein work that you have been doing on your feet.

Assembling a Team

Driving a four-in-hand is the dream of many who are enthusiastic about this sport, but requires much patient tuition before you can be considered to be a competent whip. The horses are trained singly and then in pairs before being finally put together into a team. Even though you may have the skill to do this, you must also have a team of three or four competent helpers with you when you first assemble your team and subsequently should always have two grooms with you whenever you drive out.

6 Driving Tips

Dress

Although dress and presentation will be covered more fully later, any tips on driving must be preceded by advice on what you should wear. Gloves are the main essential; unless you have rawhide skin, your fingers can very soon become sore, and gloves will also help you to grip the reins more securely. They should preferably be made of leather, unlined, and a good fit. Nothing is more tiring when driving than having too tight a pair of gloves which restrict the circulation in the fingers and make your hand movements clumsy. It is also advisable to carry a spare pair of gloves, especially in bad weather when the reins may become slippery and difficult to hold.

Two other items of dress which, although they are not essential, will make you look more workmanlike, are a driv-

Fig 73 Mark Broadbent, correctly dressed, driving his team of ponies.

ing apron and a hat. Aprons really fall into three categories: a warm one for winter, a light one for summer and a waterproof one, which is necessary all year round. The apron should buckle around your waist so that you do not have to fuss about tucking it around you when on the box seat. It should be wide enough to cover your hips when seated and long enough to reach at least your mid-calf. Modesty demands that a lady's driving apron should be somewhat more ample than a man's, but in both cases they should look tidy when you are on the vehicle. Apart from warmth and protection, a rug will cause the spare end of the reins to fall neatly to one side of your lap, where they cannot get entangled with your legs. Wearing a hat gives an added air of tidiness to your turn-out and can also be a blessing to keep your hair in place on a windy day, provided, of course, that the hat itself is sufficiently well fitting to stay on.

Mounting the Carriage

Before attempting to get on to your vehicle, check very carefully that every piece of harness is correctly adjusted and buckles are done up in the right holes. The bridle is particularly important and you should check the tightness of the noseband, throat lash and curb chain, as well as ensuring that the reins are buckled into the position in which you usually drive. Do not assume that because you fitted the harness yourself, it must be right – that is a recipe for disaster. It is all too easy to overlook something which you may have thought you had done but which could be dangerous if not corrected, so check round carefully. If you always adopt the same routine, the horse will get used to it and it will be an added safeguard that you do not miss anything out.

Having satisfied yourself that all is in order you are now ready to get into your carriage. If you have already buckled on your driving apron, pick up one of the bottom corners and tuck it into the waistband so that it will not get under your feet as you mount the vehicle. Standing on the off side, take the reins and whip in your right hand so that your left hand is free to grasp the side of the carriage or the handle that is usually positioned there and assists you as you step into the vehicle.

Once on board, sit down quickly and quietly and immediately transfer the reins to the correct position in your left hand (*see Fig 74*). Straighten your driving apron and you are now ready to drive off. The whip should be held in your right hand where it feels easily balanced, usually near the upper ferrule of the handle, and positioned so that it is at an approximate angle of forty-five degrees from the ground and forty-five degrees from your body. This will leave the thong hanging down just in front of the near side of the dashboard where it is ready for use. You should never travel with it stuck in the whip socket, 'flying like a flag of incompetence' as Sandy Watney once described it. The correct way to use a single or pair horse driving whip is with a circular movement so that the thong of the whip strikes the horse down the shoulder between the collar and the pad.

Once both you and your groom are seated in the carriage it is important to adjust the balance so that the weight on the horse's back is as light as possible.

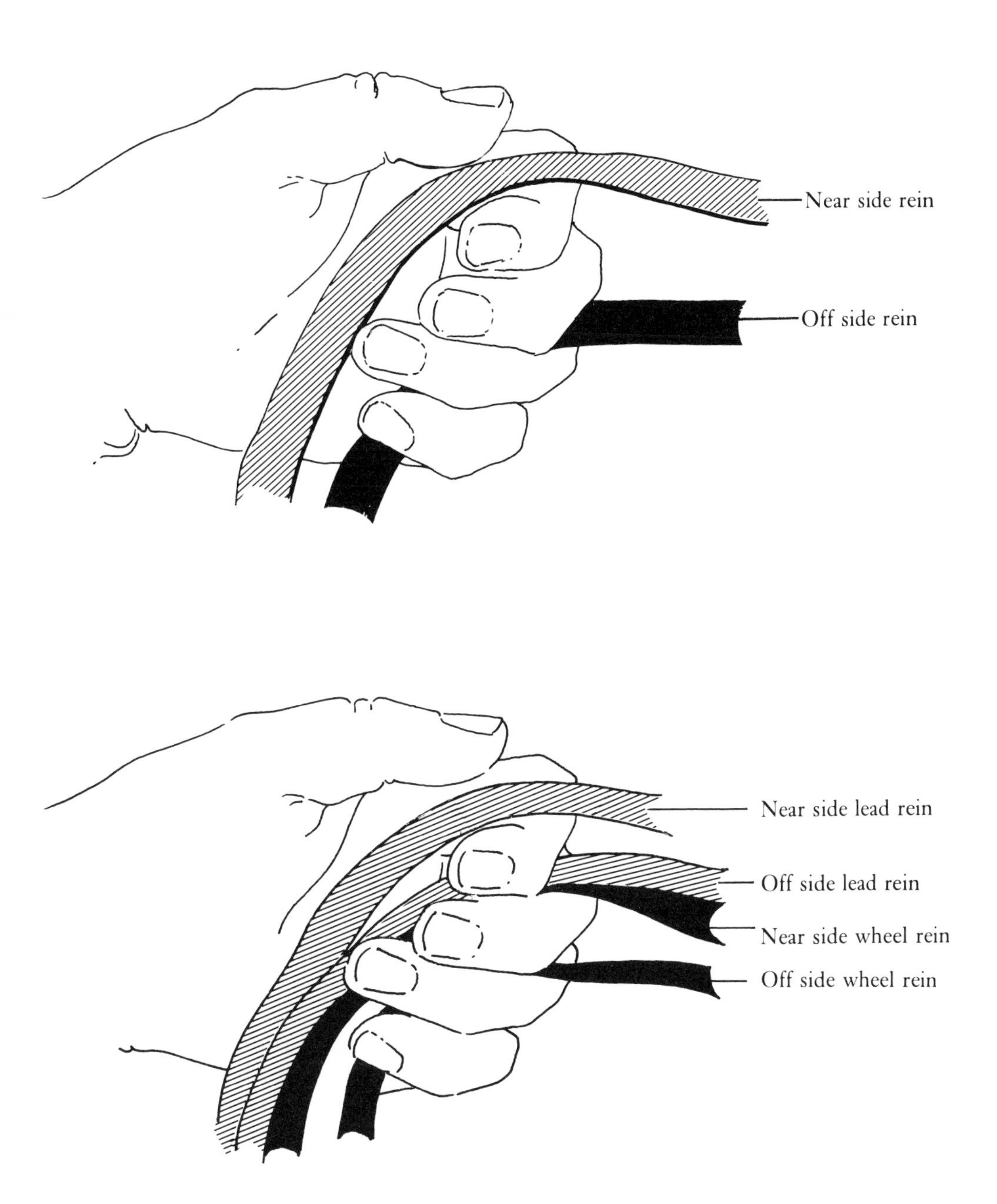

Fig 74 Hand holding two reins and hand holding four reins.

Fig 75 Claudia Bunn showing a good seat and correctly held whip.

Most single vehicles have an adjustable seat which can be moved backwards and forwards on runners, although once in the correct position it should be locked into place. This is usually done by locking pins or a screw handle positioned under the seat.

Many carriages also have an adjustable footrest to help you adopt a comfortable driving position, which is all important to enable you to exercise proper control. A firm box seat that slopes forward will help you to sit up properly with your knees slightly bent and your feet braced at the correct angle on the floor or footrest. This balancing and seat adjustment is obviously necessary the first time, but is then only required if you change your groom.

Aids

You have three aids when driving: the voice, the whip and the reins. Each of these should be used positively and properly. As when lungeing and longreining, give your commands clearly and distinctly, each one being easily differentiated. Clicking noises made with the tongue and whistling are not to be recommended, as others may do it and confuse your horse. Occasional words of encouragement let your horse know that you are still there and in command, but continual chatter only makes him lose concentration and 'switch off'. Do not shout your commands but give them in a strong clear voice, remembering that the horse's head is some ten feet (3m) away from you.

If you have occasion to use your whip, do so sharply and infrequently. Constant light taps with the whip will lose their effectiveness entirely; discipline should be administered in the same way a parent would chastise a naughty child, with a sharp rebuke which demands obedience.

Your reins are naturally the main contact between you and your horse and your handling of them is the key to the whole job. The messages that you transmit to the horse's mouth must be at the same time firm and sympathetic – strong in their intent but gentle in their operation. For driving a single horse, both reins should be held in the left hand, with the near side rein over the index finger and the off side rein between the second and third fingers. The reins then lie in the palm of the hand and the little finger is clamped down on both of them, while the thumb is pressed on to the top of the near side rein. The wrist should be vertical and rounded inwards to give flexibility, not turned outwards, which tends to lock the wrist and causes the forearm to become tired very quickly.

As soon as the horse is moving freely forward you should adjust the length of the reins by pulling them through the fingers from behind the left hand until they have an even feeling on the horse's mouth and the left hand is positioned above the left knee. Keeping the reins clamped firmly in the left hand, you will be able to slow down or speed up the pace of your horse by moving the hand backwards and forwards. All the steering should be done with the right hand, pulling the rein about ten inches (25cm) in front of the left hand. Keeping the left hand closed, once you let go of the rein that you have been pulling with the right hand, the horse will come back to a straight line. Obviously this means that whatever movement you make with the right hand, you can always bring the horse back to the same mean point of straightness. When driving through hazards some people like to have a rein in each hand, a method which in that circumstance has things to commend it, but for all other purposes the reins should be only in the left hand.

Pair Driving

When the pair have been correctly 'put to' (*see* Chapter 3) you must again check round before mounting the vehicle. As with a single, this checking should start at the near side, finishing at the off side where you will mount. As all the buckles on a pair are done up on the outside, it is easy for you to check that they are all in the correct holes and straps are in their keepers. Belly bands are easily forgotten when harnessing up, so these should be noted. Another common mistake is to fasten the reins incorrectly so that the coupling rein is on the outside, instead of crossing to the other horse. These must be carefully checked. Again, check that the rein positions on the bits are as you drive them and that the curb chains are not too tight. While at the horses' heads, check the tightness of the pole straps or pole chains. A common fault with pole straps is that they become twisted, which in time will weaken them. They should go through the rings in the pole head and kidney link in opposite directions, so that the strap lies flat.

After checking the off side horse, take up the reins and move to the point at which you are to get up on to the carriage. Holding the reins in the left

Fig 76 Correctly mounting a pair vehicle.

hand, adjust them until you can just feel the horses' mouths. Now loosen the off side rein by pulling about six inches (15cm) of rein through your fingers. Transfer the reins to the right hand and mount the vehicle quickly and quietly. Sit down and transfer the reins to your left hand, which should require little adjustment if the correct procedures outlined here have been followed. The reins should be held in the same way as for driving a single, that is with the near side rein over the index finger and off side rein between the second and third fingers.

Before moving off, make a final check that all is correct. From your position on the box seat you may now notice something that you were unable to see properly from the ground – like the incorrect positioning of the hames straps or a rein that has not been put through an inside terret.

If the vehicle is fitted with a hand-brake you should release it as you move off. Do this with the right hand, but before doing so the whip should be held under the thumb of the left hand. Many valuable whips have been damaged by a careless driver trying to release the hand-brake while still holding the whip in the right hand.

In a four-wheeled vehicle you do not have the problem of balancing your weight, but you do have the task of balancing the two horses so that they have an equal share of the work. This is done by altering the position of the coupling buckles. If the near side horse is in his collar and working while the off side horse is out of his collar, it is obvious that the latter must be moved forward. To do this you should move the coupling buckle on the off side rein back towards your hand and the coupling buckle on the near side rein forward towards the horse's head. Both should be moved the same number of holes, provided that the horses' heads are straight. If one horse is turning his head out, the coupling buckle of the other horse's rein should be moved back; similarly, if his head is turned in, his partner's coupling buckle should be moved forward. This adjustment of the reins is very important and can make the difference between the horses going properly as a pair, rather than as two horses being driven together in harness.

Once you have got the pair going well together and doing their equal share of the work, it can be the easiest of all turn-outs to drive. Keep your wrist relaxed and rounded and, if your reins are correctly adjusted, you should be able to make minor corrections of direction by moving your left hand to one side or the other. When using your right hand to steer round a corner you must let the left hand go forward slightly so that the outside horse is not held back on a corner; if anything, push the outside horse forward because he has the greater distance to travel. By constant schooling, turning in both directions, the horses will soon learn that when they are on the outside, they must stride out to make up the extra ground.

When asking a pair to stand still, take care to ensure that they do not attempt to rub their heads on the end of the pole. This could result in a very nasty accident: if the horse pulls his bridle off, not only might he take fright when he sees the vehicle to which he is attached, but without a bit in his mouth you have no control if he does 'take off'.

Before asking a pair to 'rein back' in a vehicle, they must be schooled individually and together on long reins. They

Fig 77 Richard Margrave driving a well-balanced pair.

should walk back straight when commanded, accompanied by a steady pull on the reins. Horses who have been properly schooled to rein back by a rider will soon learn to go backwards in harness. If resistance is encountered, it sometimes helps to get an assistant to tap the horse with a crop just below the knee. You should teach them to rein back about four or five strides and then stop. Do not let them run backwards in an uncontrolled fashion because that will be disastrous when they are in a vehicle. Just a few paces at a time must be the rule.

Tandem Driving

The progression from single to tandem driving is the most economical, but tandem driving requires a much greater degree of skill and dexterity. Two other essentials are a free-going leader, who will answer readily to your commands, and an agile assistant who can get to the leader's head if you get in a tangle.

When contemplating tandem driving it is important to put some extra time in with your longreining, so that your horses become very obedient to your voice. One of the best tandem leaders of recent years was a coloured mare called Carousel, driven by Sarah Garnett, who referred to her as Prue and had such a wonderful rapport with her that she could virtually control her by voice alone. Such control is only achieved by hours of patient training and this is the basis of good tandem driving. The leader's traces, which clip on to the wheeler's tug buckles, should be long enough to enable the leader to turn without interfering with the wheeler's head, but not so long that they can drop into dangerous loops around the leader's hind feet. They should also be held in trace bearers, which are positioned over the leader's hips.

The reins are held in the left hand with the near lead rein on top of the index finger and the off lead rein between the first and second fingers. The near wheel rein also goes between these two fingers, but beneath the off lead rein, while the off wheel rein goes between the second and third fingers. All four reins are then clamped into the palm by the little finger and the thumb is pressed on to the top rein. Control of these reins requires the greatest dexterity, particularly when turning, and you should practise by holding four reins in your hand until you

Fig 78 Tony Bache going well at one event . . .

Fig 79 ... and not so well at another!

are so used to the feel of them that you can pull any of them with your right hand without having to look down to see which is which.

To turn the leader to the right you should take a loop in the off lead rein and tuck it under your thumb. As the leader begins to turn, the right hand should lightly hold the near wheel rein to prevent the wheeler from jumping round after the leader, and to control him round into a smooth curve. When the leader has turned far enough you should allow the loop to slip out from under your thumb in a controlled manner, but do not just drop it. Turning to the left is done in a similar manner, with a loop in the near lead rein and checking the off wheel rein.

While this method of driving with the reins in the left hand is correct for showing and driving dressage, it is also possible to drive a tandem with two hands which, while not being so stylish, can be more positive for driving hazards and cones. As you must still hold your whip, this two-handed style does stop you from using it on your leader. The two near side reins should be buckled together and the off side reins buckled together, and these buckles should lie in the palms of your hands. The leader reins now run over the index fingers and the wheeler reins under the little fingers. It is now possible to turn both horses to the right simply by pulling with the right hand. To make this a neater movement it is best to roll the wrists in opposite directions, so that the opposing wheel rein is checked when a leader rein is pulled (*see Fig 80*).

Team Driving

Anyone contemplating driving a team is well advised to make himself conversant with single, pair and tandem driving before attempting to tackle a four-in-hand. This is because all that has been said in this chapter applies to driving a team. The configuration of reins is similar to two pairs, while the handling of the reins is similar to that for a tandem.

Checking round before driving off must be even more meticulous because there is so much that can go wrong. Experienced assistance is absolutely es-

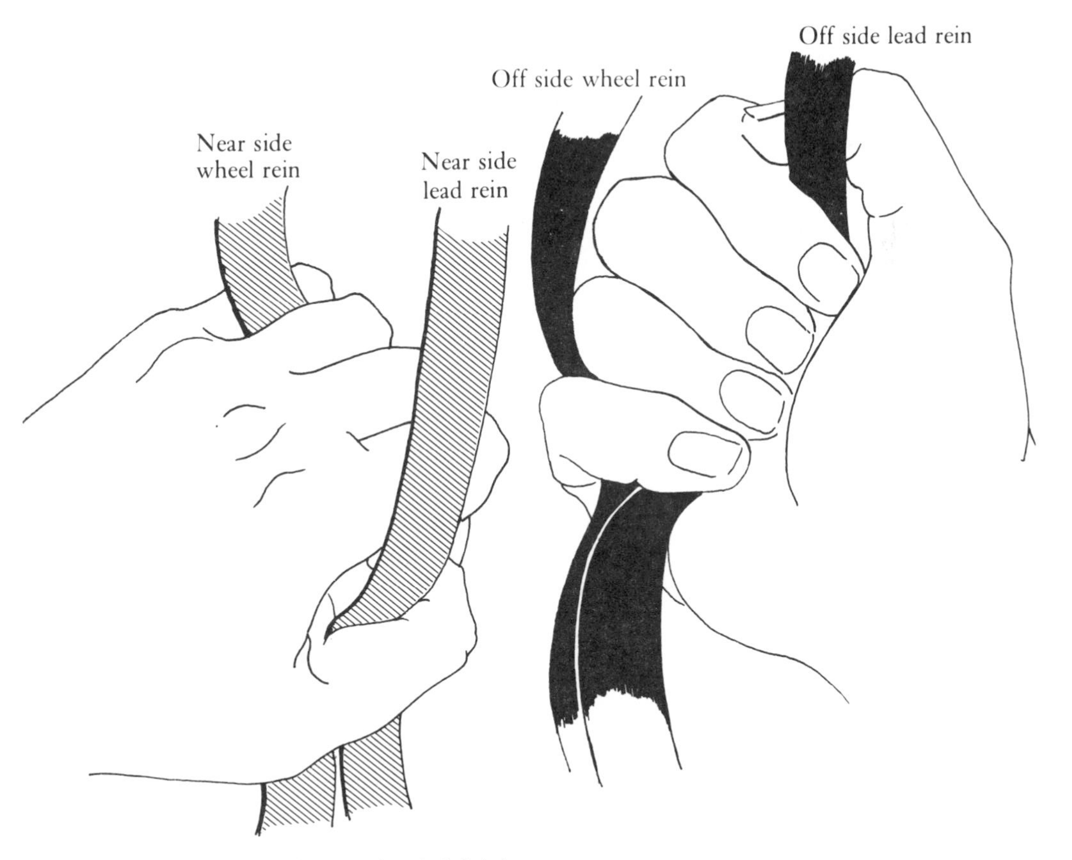

Fig 80 Rolling wrists for two-handed driving.

Fig 81 John Ravenscroft with his team of Cleveland Bays at Holker in 1984.

sential when driving a team. It is foolish to drive with less than two grooms on the carriage with you, particularly in the early stages, because if there are any adjustments to be made, either to harness or vehicle, there must always be someone to hold the horses' heads.

While accidents can happen in the best regulated establishments, every effort should be made to do things in the safest possible manner and experience is no excuse for being slapdash when putting a driving turn-out together.

7 Preparing for a Show

Once you have acquired a good horse or pony, have fitted him with harness and driven him in a vehicle, it is only natural that you will want to show him off to people, or pit his fitness and your skill against others at a driving event. Your decision to do this, and to do it properly, entails a great deal of preparation and planning so that you will enjoy the experience and be truly competitive.

The first event is always the worst, for it is this one that sets the wheels in motion, literally and metaphorically. After this you will know where the pitfalls are and what you can do to improve your competitive chances and your logistical administration at a show or event.

Nothing in this life can be attempted without a certain amount of paperwork and form filling, and carriage driving is certainly no exception. Taking a horse out in the company of others is not without its dangers, no matter how well schooled your particular animal may be, so it is important that you have some sort of insurance to cover you in case of accident. Many of the large insurance companies can arrange various types of cover to suit your requirements, but the simplest way to gain third party insurance is to become a member of the British Horse Society. Such membership gives you automatic protection, but will not cover you for loss or damage to your horse or vehicle. For this you need additional insurance with one of the many firms that advertise such protection plans in the equestrian journals. Other countries operate similar insurance schemes, organised by their national driving associations.

If you want to compete at horse driving trials in Britain, membership of the British Horse Society and the Horse Driving Trials Group is a must and your horse or pony must then be registered with them. You will be sent a registration document on application to the British Horse Society headquarters and this must then be completed by your vet. It consists of a comprehensive description of your horse or pony, together with diagrams showing his various markings, his breeding and his age. The veterinary officer will also have to certify that your animal has had a course of injections against equine influenza, a necessary precaution where horses are to be stabled in close proximity to each other, and the document will then be a permanent and constant record of any further inoculations that the horse may receive. If, at a future date, you decide to sell the horse it is good to have such proof to show a prospective purchaser. This information will also be required when completing your entry form, which is the next piece of paperwork to be tackled.

At the beginning of every driving season the Horse Driving Trials Group of the British Horse Society produces a schedule of all the national events, and this will be sent to you together with a sheaf of entry forms. Each event will specify what information they require from a prospective competitor, how much you must pay for your entry and any stabling charges. The event will acknowledge your entry and send you the necessary badges and passes in good time. They will also tell you the latest time for withdrawals in case anything should go wrong and you are unable to go.

Once your entry has been accepted, you must start your preparation. Carriage driving is a friendly sport that is enjoyed by many family groups so one of the early decisions to be made is who is actually going to the event and where they will be accommodated. If only two or three people are going they can live quite comfortably in the horse box or trailers, but if there are a greater number of helpers thought must be given as to where they will all live for the three or four days you will be away. If you intend taking a caravan to give you additional living space and cooking facilities, you must let the event organisers know this so that they can send you additional passes. They may make a small additional charge but many events allow caravans to be taken at no extra cost. Local tourist offices are helpful in supplying details of bed and breakfast accommodation in the area but this should be booked early, particularly for the bigger events at which there are likely to be many helpers. Catering details are best delegated to one member of your team so that you are free to concentrate on getting your horse and vehicle properly prepared.

Training and Fitness

For your first competition it will obviously be best to choose one that has a three-section marathon and will, therefore, be less demanding on your animal. No matter what grade of competition you choose to enter, the build-up in the horse's training must be started months earlier, as you increase the lengths of your exercise drives to prepare him for a marathon.

The two basic requirements from a competition horse are speed and stamina, and these can be improved by carefully planned exercise. Concentrate on stamina first, as you build up the lengths of your drives until he can go for 12, 16, 20 and 24 km without showing signs of distress or undue sweating. When a good standard of stamina has been achieved by quiet, relaxed drives, you can improve his speed over sections of your route, punctuating the fast phases with walks and halts in the same manner as you will need to do on the marathon.

Obviously with the increase in exercise he will need more to eat, and as horses' diets and appetites vary it is not possible to say exactly what feed should be given, but any mixture should have a generous helping of oats.

The horse's general health must be carefully observed and any signs of soreness caused by collars, cruppers, or girth should be swiftly attended to. Swabbing down his shoulder with a little alum solution or surgical spirit will often strengthen the skin and stop any soreness, but if any of the harness is continually chafing it must be altered or replaced. Shoeing must be checked every morning when the feet are picked out to ensure that the shoes are tight and that none of the clenches are standing proud from the hoof when they may cause injury to another leg.

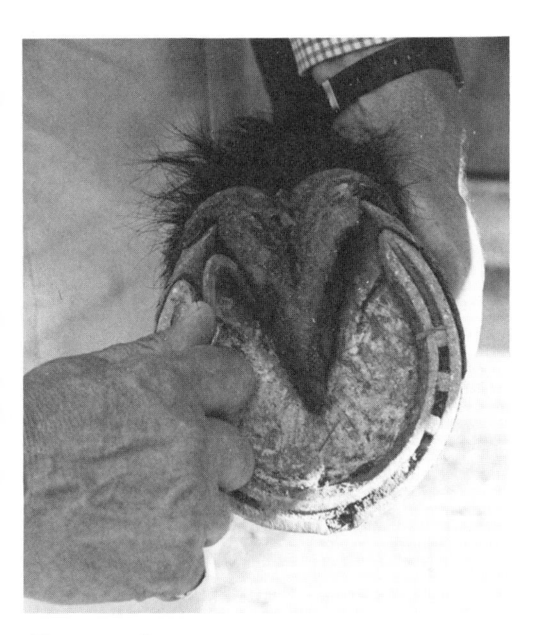

Fig 82 Cleaning and checking feet and shoes.

Dressage Practice

Your training drives should be done in the harness and vehicle that you will actually be using for the competition. Practice is valueless if you then do something entirely different when you get to the event. This also applies to your dressage practice which you should do in your best vehicle and best harness several times before taking it to a competition.

Practising dressage should not be a daily exercise but something that you do two or three times a week. It requires a high degree of concentration from both you and your horse. Each particular movement should be practised until you are certain that you are doing it at the correct pace and in the proper shape for the figure. You do not need a full-size dressage arena to practise 20 or 30-metre circles, but any area that you do use should be correctly marked out so that both you and your horse can see the right markers. Horses sometimes shy away from the white boards of an arena so it will be a help if you can find some alongside which you can drive, keeping your vehicle wheels as close as is comfortable to the boards.

Dressage tests must be driven from memory and must therefore be well learned beforehand. This can be done without actually using your horse and vehicle, by the simple expedient of writing the dressage letters on pieces of paper, laying them on the floor of a suitable room and then walking around this makeshift arena. At first you can walk round reading the test from a book or dressage sheet so that you know where the changes of pace take place, but after a while you can dispense with the crib and walk round reciting the test to yourself.

Another useful hint for learning dressage is to draw each separate movement to scale on a sheet of graph paper. In this way you will see the exact shape of the figures that you will be required to drive and the way in which they connect to the next.

Preparing the Vehicle

When beginning showing or competitive driving you will probably have only one vehicle which is in daily use for exercise until a day or two before the event. The final cleaning must therefore be left until the last minute, but a certain amount of work should be done earlier. The spare equipment that you are going to carry can be well cleaned and laid out neatly in a wooden box, tray, or basket and then put into the carriage when you arrive at the competition. Wheel bearings should be checked for tightness and greased or oiled according to the type of wheel. If the vehicle that you are showing is an old one, you may find a leather washer at the back of the wheel has become old and compressed, so making the wheel loose on the axle. It must be replaced and the wheel tightened so that there is no rattle as you drive along.

All nuts and bolts on the vehicle should be regularly checked for tightness, especially just before you leave for an event where you may be driving over some fairly rough terrain. Once all the mechanical checks have been done, you can spend an evening touching up the paintwork. This should be done carefully, with a small brush, and using the correct colour to blend in with the original. The parts that will need most attention are the springs and these should be well cleaned off, removing all dirt, grease and traces of rust before finally wiping them down with a little white spirit on a soft cloth. The touch up paint can then be carefully applied and when that is dry a coat of clear varnish will help it all blend together. The last part to be painted are the steps which are in constant use right up to the competition and can be painted the day before the event with some quick-drying paint. The upholstery should be thoroughly cleaned with a cleaner suitable for the material. If it is leather, or leather cloth, it can easily be cleaned with one of the popular brands of spray furniture polish, but care must be taken to ensure that all the dirt is first removed from seams and buttoning. Ribbed rubber matting in a vehicle looks very smart when it is clean but can spoil the overall

Fig 83 Touching up the paintwork before an event.

effect completely if left muddy. Just washing is not sufficient; it must be thoroughly cleaned with black shoe polish and a stiff shoe brush.

The lamps can be cleaned well in advance and then wrapped in a soft cloth until they are needed. Before you clean them, touch up any paintwork that may have become chipped, particularly where the stem sits in the lamp bracket.

The cleaning of all brass work on the vehicle, such as rein rails and shaft fittings, should be left until the night before the competition or done early in the morning if you have enough time before your class, so that it all looks fresh and bright, and not tarnished.

Preparing Horse and Harness

In the weeks before an event you should make sure that your horse or pony is quite prepared to travel in whatever transport you are intending to use. If he is a reluctant loader, experiment by putting his feed bucket on the ramp of the horse box or trailer, moving it higher up with each successive feed until you are actually feeding him standing in the position in which he will be travelling. Do not leave the bucket loose where he can pull it down or tip it over, but secure it in a safe way so that he is obliged to walk on the ramp to reach his feed.

The horse preparing to travel needs to wear leg bandages; he should be accustomed to having these put on and should be walked round the stable yard in them a few times so that he is used to having a firm support around his legs. Tail bandaging should not present a problem as you will have been using them in your grooming to get the tail hairs lying correctly at the top of the tail. Tail bandages have a habit of being rubbed and slipping down when travelling, so should always be used in conjunction with a tailguard.

Horses' feet are always closely scrutinised by judges and a good clean with a stiff brush, inside and out, should be part of your daily grooming, so that they only require some light hoof oil on the day to show them to their best advantage.

Harness can be brought up to standard over the preceding weeks, checking carefully for any weakened straps that need the attention of a harness maker. This particularly applies to the harness that you have been using every day and now intend to use for the cross-country drive. Do not assume that because you have been using it every day, it must be all right; you will not have been subjecting it to the stress that it is liable to have put upon it in competition and it is then that any weakness will let you down. If you are able to have two sets of harness, one for showing and one for everyday and cross-country use, so much the better, but if you are starting off with just one set of harness, get a show set first and gradually build up your working set by purchasing odd items that you can get at sales or from the advertisement columns of equestrian magazines. Very soon you will then have the two sets that you require and can keep your show harness in tiptop condition.

When cleaning your best harness you should first undo all the buckles, making notes, if necessary, on a piece of paper of the holes into which the various pieces should be done up. All brasses should then be thoroughly cleaned, not forgetting the backs of the buckles. Metal polish

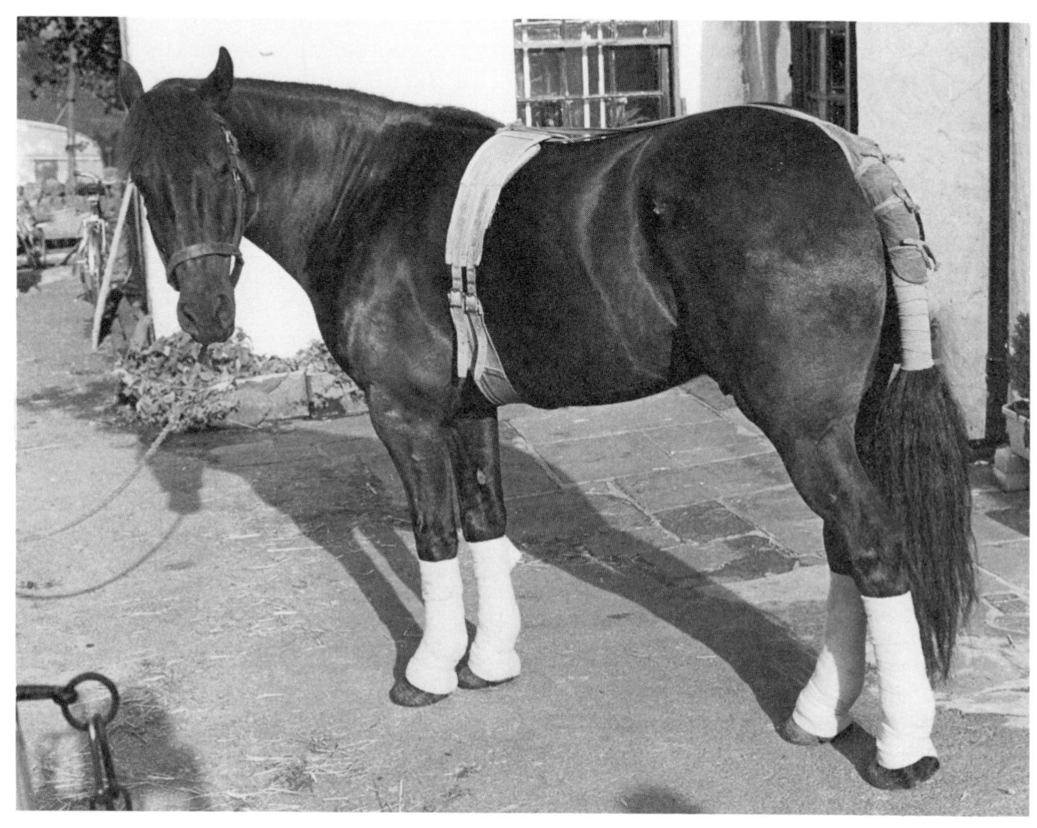

Fig 84 Pony prepared to travel.

is not magic and simply putting it on and wiping it off will not produce a shine – a generous use of elbow grease is also required. The insides of the leather parts coming into contact with the horse should be sponged off with warm water to remove all the dirt and then have saddle soap rubbed well into them. The fronts and sides of the leatherwork should then be cleaned with black polish. Using the tip of the blacking brush you should rub the blacking well into the parts of the leather that have been affected by metal polish. Do not worry too much if it goes on to the brass that you have already cleaned because a quick rub with a soft cloth will soon remove any surplus polish. The edges of the leatherwork are most important because anyone standing in front of your horse will be looking straight at them. Should they become rough or furry they can be smoothed down by rubbing them with beeswax and then brown paper, to seal them and make them polishable once more.

Driving reins are always brown and should remain that way. After removing dirt and sweat with warm water, a good rub down with saddle soap should be all that they need. If you have got white marks from the metal polish around the billet these can be camouflaged with a little brown shoe polish.

When your harness is clean it should be wrapped in a soft cloth and carefully packed in its travelling box. Put the heaviest items, such as the collar, at the bottom and the lightest at the top so that nothing has a great weight on it that may mark it. Check it as you pack it and make sure that any items such as the curb chain are not left out.

Check-lists

There are so many things to remember when setting out for a show or event that to rely on your memory alone is to court disaster. It is far better to draw up check-lists for all that you need to take and these can be kept in a folder for reference before setting out each time. The suggested headings for these lists are:

1. Driver's clothes, including hat, gloves and whip.
2. Groom's clothes for both presentation and cross country.
3. Harness (both sets listed, piece by piece).
4. Vehicle or vehicles (with spares itemised).
5. Forage.
6. Food (for driver, groom and helpers).
7. Paperwork (including badges, tickets and map).
8. Stable equipment (including bandages, rugs, grooming kit and cleaning kit).

Having drawn up these lists which hopefully will include all that you need to take with you, be sure to consult them frequently during your preparation and packing. The last thing to check in your preparation is your transport and stabling arrangements. If you are using a trailer, make sure that it will fit on to the vehicle that is to tow it and that the lights can be plugged in so that they work correctly. If your transport is a horse box, ensure that the batteries are fully charged and that it has enough fuel to start when you need it. Nothing is more frustrating than finding that your lorry will not start on the final day after months of preparation.

If you are taking temporary stabling, make sure that it is complete and in good working order. Stow it on your vehicle in such a way that you will be able to get at it without having to disturb everything else. When arriving at the event this will be the first thing to be erected and so should be readily accessible.

With everything checked and ready, you are now off to put those long hours of preparation to the test.

8 Presentation and Dressage

Presentation

Over recent years there has been a move by the European members of the FEI to dispense with, or severely curtail, this phase of the three-day driving competition. Their reasoning is that there is a great disparity of national dress amongst competitors at international events, and judges tend to favour that with which they are more familiar. The fact that British competitors have always done very well at this phase of the competition has been due to hard work and attention to detail by competitors and judges alike. Presentation judges were, in the first instance, drawn from the ranks of the Coaching Club who have a long tradition of excellence in turning out four-in-hands, and this rather irked those who felt that their standards were unreasonably severe. Over the years, however, the arguments have dwindled as competitors have come nearer to the excellent standard for which those early judges were looking. Judges have also become better educated regarding what they should be inspecting and the points that can be classified as nit-picking. The senior judges who control events in the roles of President of the Ground Jury or Technical Delegate are quick to point out to junior judges which of their remarks may be construed as going into unnecessary detail. It is now the practice for Open Classes to have their presentation judged as part of the dressage test, on the move, whilst Novice Classes still retain a static presentation judged separately prior to their dressage.

The form on which the presentation judges enter their scores and remarks is divided into five sections (*see Fig 85*) and in each of these a maximum of 10 marks may be given. When totalled, the score is added to that of the other presentation judges and is divided by the number of those judges to give an average mark. This mark is subtracted from 50 and the resulting figure is divided by five to arrive at the number of presentation penalty points. This last division by five is to ensure that the effect of the presentation mark is correct, balanced against the other phases of the competition.

Driver and Groom

Looking at each of the categories in turn, the first is the dress and appearance of the driver and groom. When deciding what to wear, due consideration should be given to the type of carriage that you intend to drive. For instance, the country carts, such as the Norfolk or Essex carts, require a country type of dress, rather than the suit and top hat that should be worn with the more formal gigs and phaetons. If the driver is wearing a tweed suit and bowler hat, his groom should be similarly dressed in what is usually known as 'stable livery'. This consists of a suit, often of the pepper-and-salt variety that was issued to grooms as part of their emoluments, a bowler hat of the same style and colour as the driver's, a

JUDGING SHEET
Competition A – Section I
PRESENTATION

COMPETITOR NO .....

TO BE JUDGED		MARKS 1 – 10	REMARKS
1. Driver, Groom and Passengers	Position, dress, hat, gloves, holding whip, handling of horses.		
2. Horses	Condition, turn out, cleanliness, matching, condition of shoeing.		
3. Harness	Condition, proper fit, cleanliness.		
4. Vehicle	Condition, cleanliness, height of pole and spare equipment.		
5. General Impression	Whole turnout.		
	TOTAL PRESENTATION		

SIGNATURE OF JUDGE ....

Fig 85 Presentation judges' scorecard.

pair of strong shoes or boots and brown leather gloves. It would be rather Victorian to expect the groom to wear a stiff collar, so a smart collar and suitable tie will suffice.

If the driver is wearing a dark suit and a top hat, his groom should be dressed in conventional livery – boots with brown tops, white breeches, livery coat, stock and collar and black top hat. Points for which the judges will be looking in this form of dress are that the boots are clean and well fitting; that the breeches, if they have buttons, button on the outside of the knee and not on the inside as with hunting breeches, although in these days of stretch fabrics most breeches do not have any buttons at all; that the livery coat fits well and reaches to about six inches (15 cm) above the knee, having five or six buttons on the front and six on the back; that the collar is stiff but without wings; that the stock, which is usually of the 'Newmarket Tie' style, is correctly fastened with a stock pin; and that the top hat, which is often neglected, has been properly 'dressed' to make it shine.

A smart costume is usually the tidiest and most attractive dress for a lady whip, avoiding anything which could be regarded as 'fancy dress', but a small word

Fig 86 HRH The Duke of Edinburgh correctly wearing country livery to drive his team of ponies, with his grooms suitably attired.

Fig 87 Alwyn Holder in dark suit and top hat with his grooms in full livery.

Fig 88 Amanda Royce smartly dressed to drive her pair of horses.

of warning – make sure that your driving rug is considerably longer than your skirt. One elderly gentleman judge was covered in confusion when he lifted up a lady's driving apron and picked up her skirt with it. A pair of sensible shoes with low heels will give you greater comfort and confidence when driving; and the whole ensemble should be crowned with a close fitting hat. A happy medium can usually be achieved, avoiding too masculine a form of dress and a too fussy femininity.

The dress for female grooms has fallen into a pattern and now consists of black boots (without garter straps), white breeches, black jacket, white shirt and suitable tie, and a velvet riding cap.

If a driver chooses to carry a passenger instead of a groom, he should have a knee apron to match the driver's and should

Fig 89 A lady groom adds the final touches.

stay seated while the turn-out is being inspected. This applies mainly to single turn-outs because the tandems, pairs and teams should have grooms to assist them.

Horse

Second on the judge's list is the presentation of the horse. Here he will be looking at the suitability of the animal for the carriage that he is being asked to pull, that is, that he is not too big or too small for the height or size of the vehicle. His condition can generally be ascertained by the state of his coat and the way in which he is standing. An alert-looking horse with a clean and well-groomed coat that has a good shine, or 'bloom', to it will obviously score better than a dull-looking animal.

Plaiting of manes, if done well, can show off a well-held neck and head, but tails are best left unplaited and full at the top so that when carried they fall neatly to cover the crupper. With native breeds, where the manes are left unplaited they should be well combed and any straggling ends removed. Fetlocks on these breeds are untrimmed but should be cleaned and brushed; those whose fetlocks are trimmed should have it neatly done and there should be no harsh line where the trimming finishes and the full coat begins. Ergots and chestnuts should not be long and this is usually a job for the farrier's sharp knife. The standard of shoeing is also taken into consideration, along with the cleanliness of the feet. The hooves should be well scrubbed and lightly oiled and, while lacquer is decried, black polish can make the feet look smarter. Conformation is not a consideration but obviously if a horse is well put together he will be more pleasing to the judge's eye than one who is oddly shaped.

Harness

See Chapter 3 for a detailed discussion of harness and its preparation. It is worth stressing, however, that when cleaning it for competition, you should polish the edges of the leather, as these are most obvious when the horse is wearing it. If these edges become fluffy it is a good idea to rub them with some beeswax and then brown paper which will smooth and seal them.

The items of spare harness required to be carried on each vehicle are listed in the driving trials rules and these should be easily accessible, well laid out, and clean. Some people try to impress the judges by the amount of spares they carry, but usually finish up looking like a tinker's cart. A simple layout of the items required is much more impressive, as well as being easier to check. Admittedly when you are going on a marathon it is a good idea to carry spare cord or baler twine, a sharp knife, some bandages and a selection of straps and various tools, but none of these need be in the vehicle during the presentation phase.

Vehicle

The inspection of the vehicle should concentrate on its cleanliness and suitability, with little regard to whether it is traditional or modern. A good judge should not be influenced by the amount of money spent on the vehicle, but by the care and attention to detail with which it is presented. Paintwork should be free from all dirt and rust, particularly around the springs, where such things are usually evident, and any chips should have been carefully touched up. The bright metal fittings should be of the same metal as the harness furniture, with the exception of the pole head and swingletree ends of a team vehicle which are usually of bright steel or chrome plate.

Lamps should be of a suitable size and pattern for the vehicle and fit properly into the sockets. Carriages should have rear lamps or reflectors mounted in a suitable place where they will not be obscured by any part of the vehicle or by a groom seated on the back.

General Impression

The last mark is for general impression and, although each of the previous items judged may be very good in isolation, this is where they are marked in relation to each other. A driver and groom may themselves be beautifully turned out, but if they are too big for the pony vehicle they will lose marks. Similarly, the position of the horse in relation to the vehicle could make a difference to the overall look of the turn-out. If the Europeans win the presentation debate, this general impression may be all that is left of presentation in international competition and so should be considered at the very outset – when you are first deciding what horse and carriage will be most suited to you.

Dressage

While driven dressage originates from the ridden format, the movements have had to be drastically adapted because of the restriction of harness and vehicle. Thus the object of the tests, specified in the rules, is to judge the freedom and regularity of paces, harmony, impulsion, suppleness, lightness, ease of movement, and the correct positioning of horses on the move. The driver is also judged on his style, accuracy and general command of his horse or team. Where more than one horse is driven, that is, in pairs, tandems or teams, they are judged on the way that they move together and not as individual animals.

In order to discover what is really required of the horse in dressage tests it is best to study the description of paces that have been laid down by the FEI. Although these were written for the guidance of riders in the first instance, the points below are those applicable to driven dressage.

The Halt

At the halt the horse should stand attentive, motionless and straight, with his weight evenly distributed over all four legs and ready to move off on command. The neck is raised, the poll high, the head a little in front of the vertical and the mouth light. The horse should be gently champing the bit and maintaining a light contact with the driver's hand.

The transition from any pace to the halt should be made in a smooth precise movement.

The Walk

This is a marching pace in which the four legs of the horse follow one another in four-time, well marked and evenly maintained. When the four beats cease to be well defined, even and regular, the walk is disunited or broken. The horse should walk energetically but calmly, with even and determined steps distinctly marking four equally spaced beats. The hind feet should touch the ground slightly in front of the footprints of the forefeet.

The Trot

This is a two-time pace, on alternate diagonals (near fore and off hind, off fore and near hind), separated by a moment of suspension. It should always be entered without hesitation and with free, active and regular steps. The quality of the trot is judged by the general impression, the elasticity and regularity of the steps while maintaining impulsion and the same cadence. Three types of trot are required in driven dressage: the collected, working and extended trots.

In the working trot the horse shows itself properly balanced and on the bit, going forward with even, elastic steps and a good hock action. The head is held slightly forward of vertical.

For the collected trot the horse should have a more rounded outline, with the head held in and the neck raised, enabling the shoulders to move with greater ease. The hocks should be well engaged and maintain energetic impulsion despite a

Fig 90 John Rogers' pair at a working trot.

slower movement. The horse's steps are shorter but he should be lighter and more mobile.

When doing an extended trot the horse covers as much ground as possible. He lengthens his stride while remaining on the bit with a light contact. The neck is lowered and extended and greater impulsion from the quarters gives a longer stride without his action becoming higher.

The best way to train horses in the different paces is to ride them, while at the same time using words of command that the horse will come to associate with the pace at which he is required to move. Any competent rider should be able to achieve this by the use of hand and leg, and after a while will be able to get the horse to extend or collect with the use of hand and voice alone. If you are unable to ride your horse, much can be achieved on long reins with the judicious use of trotting poles. By varing the distance between these the horse can be persuaded to lengthen or shorten his stride. These changes must also be co-ordinated to specific commands.

Fig 91 Mrs Jill Holah's pony showing extension.

The Rein Back

The rein back is a kind of walk backwards, the legs being raised and set down in diagonal pairs. The hind legs must remain in line and the horse must be ready to halt on command, remaining at all times lightly on the bit and well balanced.

The movement should be smooth and unhurried and the hind quarters kept in a straight line without any lowering or spreading. Any violent action on the part of the driver can have disastrous results when asking the horses to rein back in the carriage, and many a good dressage test has been spoilt by a bad movement. The three metres that is usually required for a rein back should be worked up to gradually until the horse moves quietly backwards, straight and with no resistance. He should also halt on command and move smoothly forward after a fractional pause.

The Arena and Judges

Although the lettering for dressage arenas is the same for both ridden and driven tests, the size of the driven arena must necessarily be larger. The full-size arena used for teams and tandems measures 100 metres by 40 metres, while singles and pairs perform in an arena 80 metres by 40 metres. The letters are actually places approximately three feet (90cm) behind the boards and the actual point is marked by a white post two foot six inches (85cm) high placed immediately behind the boards. Although for international competitions the line of boards must be continuous, it is permissible for club and national events to have evenly spaced gaps, thus not using so many. This is helpful in events which have so many competitors that it is necessary to run two or more arenas simultaneously.

The presiding judge is usually seated at C and if there is a panel of three judges the other two are positioned at B and E. In international competitions where five judges are employed they are positioned at R, S, V, and P, with the President again at C. He alone is responsible for the correct conduct of the test and will stop any competitor who makes an error in the course and direct him to restart at a suitable place. For an error of course, or if a groom dismounts, the President will award penalties as follows:

First incident – 5 penalties
Second incident – 10 penalties
Third incident – 15 penalties
Fourth incident – elimination

Only if the whole turn-out leaves the arena is the competitor eliminated, but if some part of the turn-out crosses the boards, the marks awarded by the judges for the particular movement in which the incident occurs will take this into consideration. The President will also stop any competitor if he considers his horse to be markedly lame, and may ask for the animal to be seen by a veterinary officer before being allowed to continue.

At the end of the test the total points awarded by each judge are added together and divided by the number of judges. These points are then deducted from the maximum of 160 allowed for the the test and they then become penalty points. To these are added any penalty points that may have been awarded by the President of the Jury for the incidents described.

Training for Dressage Movements

The starting point for both the horse and the driver when beginning driven dressage must be to learn to change pace correctly and on a marker. In order to achieve this you should first walk your horse around the arena, keeping about a foot (30cm) away from the boards and getting as tight into the corners as your vehicle will comfortably allow you to. This will establish in your mind, and to an extent in your horse's mind, the track that must be followed. When you are confident that you can drive straight down the sides of the arena, it is time to begin to change pace.

The easiest of transitions is from a walk to a working trot, and this you should do first along the side of the arena, when your horse's nose reaches the marker at E. It is most important to remember that all changes of pace and direction must take place when the horse's nose reaches the marker. Trot round the track, keeping the same distance from the boards as you did at the walk, until you reach the marker at C and then come back to a walk. Continue round the track to B, where you commence a working trot once again to A, then revert to a walk. This exercise should be repeated, dividing the arena into quarters like this until a smooth transition can be achieved, both to the trot and to the walk.

As you progress, you can do the same exercise changing from a working trot to a collected trot, but an extended trot is best attempted on the diagonals between H and F, and M and K. This gives your horse a greater feeling of freedom, as he will hopefully go forward more confidently without the boards restricting him on one side. When attempting an extended trot it is important to have your horse balanced and lined up on the marker towards which you are heading before asking him to extend. If you slightly exaggerate the slowness of pace at the beginning and end of an extension this might have the effect of making the judge think that the extension was far better than it really was.

Turns and Circles

Many of the movements in driven dressage are based on a 20-metre circle and so this is the first figure to be learned before going on to do any tests.

The distance between markers should be firmly imprinted on your mind so that you know exactly where you should drive. Many people drive around the arena looking intently at their horse's ears instead of looking at the markers which are there to assist them in driving perfect figures.

Presuming that you are practising in a smaller size arena, 80 metres by 40 metres, you should attempt your 20-metre circles in each corner. This means that the lines containing your circles are the side and end of the arena, the centre line, and an imaginary line across the arena five metres short of the line R–S, or V–P, depending at which end of the arena you are. When driving these circles it helps to think of them as squares, so that you remain straight along the edges and you should always be looking at the next side down which you have to drive. When changing rein at either G or D, both your horse and vehicle should be straight on the centre line (*see Fig 93*).

Having got these 20-metre circles

Fig 92 HRH The Duke of Edinburgh cornering in the dressage test.

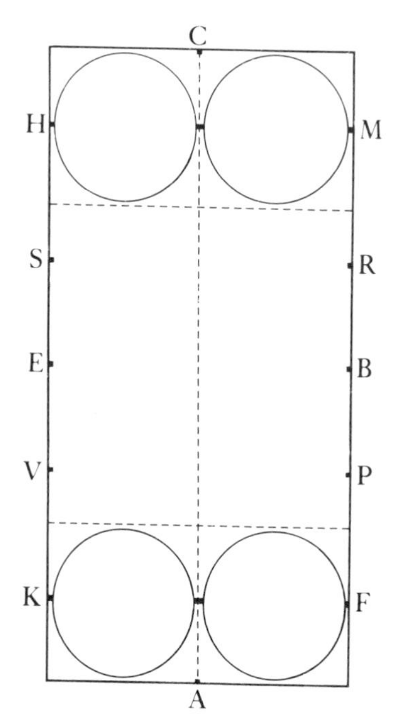

Fig 93 Dressage circles in arena corners.

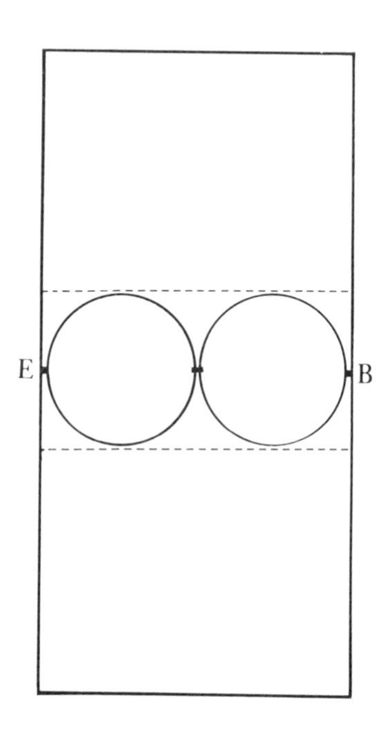

Fig 94 Dressage circles at E and B.

clearly in your mind, the next step is to practise them at B and E, where you have not got the end of the arena as a guide. This time the imaginary lines to be touched are five metres the other side of the lines R–S and V–P (*see Fig 94*). This exercise will be useful when driving a Novice test.

Now you can combine both these exercises so that you execute a circle in one corner, then drive across the arena to a circle on the centre marker, and finally do another circle in the other corner (*see Fig 95*). You will notice that when doing this you are making up ten metres on the diagonal when crossing each of the lines R–S and V–P and so you use the full 80-metre length of the arena. This has now developed into the separate movement that is required when driving the Number 3 Advanced dressage test in a smaller arena (*see Fig 96*).

Having mastered 20-metre circles, you should now turn your attention to 30-metre circles which you will be required to perform at A and C in the Advanced test. Bearing in mind that the arena is 40 metres wide this means that the sides of your circle (which you should once again think of as a square) will touch a line five metres in from either side of the arena and five metres across the lines R–S and V–P. If you walk the movement at first it will give you the time to concentrate on your exact position in relation to the markers before driving the movement as a trot, using both hands to steer your horse through the correct figure.

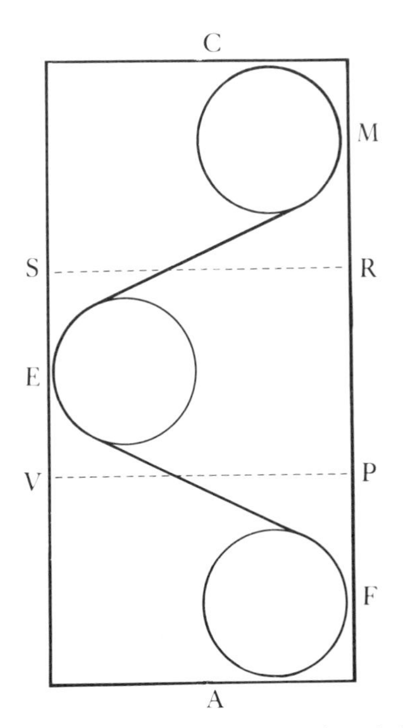

Fig 95 Dressage circles using the whole arena.

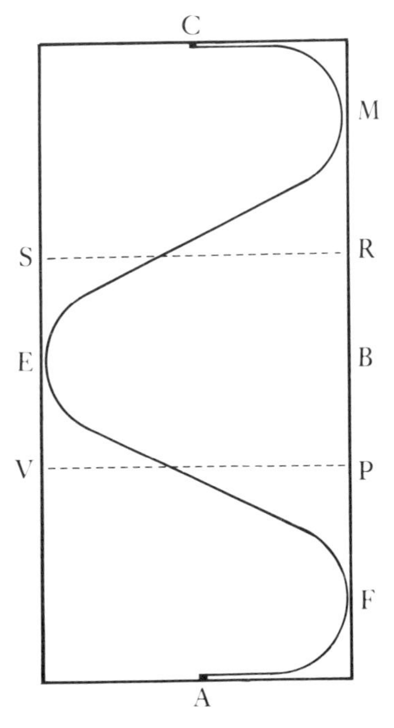

Fig 96 Movement for the Advanced dressage test.

One-handed Driving

Although there is no rule that requires a competitor to drive with the reins in one hand, except for the 30-metre circles in the Number 3 Advanced dressage test, it is the correct English style of driving, with the reins held as described in Chapter 6 (*see Fig 74*). The advantage of this style is that, if the reins are correctly adjusted so that the horse or horses are running straight and there is an even feel on both sides of the horse's mouth, it should be much easier to keep the horse balanced and on a straight line. Turns and circles can then be effected by using the right hand, and experienced drivers can know which rein to pull without having to look down at them. With a well-schooled horse or pair of horses, it should be possible to achieve a deviation by a simple turning of the left wrist; for example, if the thumb is turned towards you it should have the effect of tightening the near side rein and loosening the off side rein, while turning the thumb away from you has the opposite result. The movement can be emphasised by bringing the hand across the body in the opposite direction from that in which you want the horse to turn. In this way it should be easy to control a horse, or pair of horses, when driving a 30-metre circle with the reins in one hand.

Tandems and teams pose a slightly different problem because in order to get the whole turn-out describing a perfect arc it is necessary to take a loop in your

Fig 97 George Bowman doing a one-handed circle.

leader rein, which is tucked under the thumb of your left hand, while the opposing wheeler rein is kept tight by a twisting of the wrist, to prevent the wheelers coming round too quickly and cutting the circle short.

When doing a one-handed movement in a dressage test it always looks more impressive if the right hand with the whip is held out to the side at arm's length, giving an air of confidence even though you may be just about to make the biggest tangle possible – at least you will be doing it with style.

Driving with a rein in each hand, or two reins in each hand, used to be synonymous with the draymen of Carter Paterson, but since then the Hungarians have proved the effectiveness of two-handed driving for marathons (*see* Chapter 9).

9 The Marathon

After the hours of polishing and preparation for the presentation and the severe concentration required for the dressage test, the marathon phase comes as a relaxing relief. It is by far the most exciting phase of the competition and to drivers, grooms and spectators alike it is surely the most enjoyable. Added to all this, it is the most important because over its five sections many points can be lost or won to redeem or improve the dressage scores of the previous day.

The object of the marathon is to test the fitness and stamina of the horses and the ability of the driver to judge the pace at which he drives in such a way as to ensure that his horse is always fit enough to tackle the next section. There are five sections, lettered A to E, making a course of between 23 and 27 kilometres. Maximum speeds and distances are laid down for these sections.

Novice drivers are usually only required to drive three sections, A, D, and E, and the times for ponies are more lenient than those quoted below.

In the last section, E, there is a series of hazards through which the competitor must drive as quickly as possible. The maximum number of these hazards is eight (the minimum being five) and they can be either natural, for example a group of trees, or man-made, for example a series of post and rail fences. The gates in these obstacles are lettered in sequence and must measure at least 2.5 metres wide. Water obstacles are often included but these must not be deeper than 40 centimetres and must have a firm bottom. Where these are positioned on the edges of rivers, post and rail fences must be erected to prevent the horses striking out into deeper water with very dampening, if not disastrous, results.

Course Components and Design

The designing and building of the hazards is a very skilful business, particularly in national and club events where the design must be such that it proves a problem to single ponies at one end of the spectrum and teams of horses at the other. The course builder must also be able to judge which of his posts must be the stronger and most firmly in the ground, as it will

Section	Maximum Distance		Pace	Maximum Average Speed
A	10	kilometres	Any	15 k.p.h.
B	1.2	kilometres	Walk	7 k.p.h.
C	4	kilometres	Trot	20 k.p.h.
D	1.2	kilometres	Walk	7 k.p.h.
E	10	kilometres	Trot	14 k.p.h.

be round those that the competitors will be making the tightest turns. There must also be several options at each hazard so that the more ambitious can take a difficult, short route while the more cautious elect for a longer, easier journey. While it is not pleasant to see a horse or horses getting tangled in too tight a hazard, neither is it safe for the hazard to be too open and free flowing, where a driver may be tempted to go too fast and have a nasty tip up.

When planning a marathon course, the designer must also have due regard to the ground conditions over each section of the course. He must make sure that, as near as possible, the going will remain the same whatever the weather, so that there will be no appreciable difference between the first competitor to drive it and the last, who could be following in the tracks of more than a hundred vehicles.

Having decided on a route, the builder must then clearly signpost it so that no one will get lost. This is done by a series of arrows placed along the route (*see Fig 98*) just before a turn, and again just after the turn to indicate to the driver that he is still on the correct route. These arrows are mounted on posts in the ground, on

Fig 98 A turning arrow.

Fig 99 The author's daughter, Debbie, setting out on a marathon. Crash hats are recommended.

gateposts or trees, and are best placed at such a height or position that they cannot be vandalised and turned to point the wrong way by someone with a mischievous mind. As large parts of the course are driven without the competitor having seen them beforehand, it is important for the course builder to have a last look round before the first competitor starts, just to make sure that all these markers are in place. His vehicle usually carries a large supply of arrows because it is the modern practice for bigger events to sign each section with a different coloured disc to avoid confusion, particularly where one might cross or run close to another.

At certain points along the route it is

Fig 100 Ian Gilbert at Floors Castle.

often necessary to have pairs of flags, one red and one white, through which the driver must pass, keeping the white flag on the left and the red on the right. These are usually placed where there is a possibility of a competitor taking a short cut, and failure to pass through these flags can lead to elimination. Such pairs of flags are numbered consecutively and where referees are carried on the larger pair and team vehicles, they must check off the numbers as they pass them. Watching the competitors through these flags is also part of the duties of ground referees, who are employed to watch the classes that do not carry referees on their vehicles (*see Fig 101*).

Fig 101 Numbered turning flags.

Fig 102 Louise Ruffe going well.

Fig 103 Francis Millner tackles the water.

Fig 104 Rodney Ousbey in his patent 'chariot'.

Fig 105 John Bowman gets it wrong.

A course designer at Floors castle one year omitted an important pair of turning flags which meant that an unscrupulous driver could have taken a short cut straight across the Duke of Roxburghe's front lawn. Thankfully, for the future well-being of the sport, no one was rash enough to do so.

If there are particularly steep or tricky parts on the course they may be designated as being 'any pace'. This means that at these points drivers do not have to maintain a trot, but may walk or canter their horses as the terrain demands. In point of fact, this may be phased out in the near future if certain factions of the driving world are listened to. They advocate the introduction of an any pace section to replace section A, the onus then being on the driver to come in at the correct time, having driven his horses sensibly enough for them still to be fit for the remainder of the course.

The walk sections are usually on a fairly flat stretch of ground, although slight gradients are permissible. After each of the walk sections, there is a compulsory halt of ten minutes when the horses are checked by a veterinary officer to ensure that they are not exhausted or distressed. After a ten-minute walk and a ten-minute rest any horse or pony should be well recovered and ready to get going again, but if the veterinary officer considers that a longer rest is necessary there should always be a judge there to implement this.

Section C is a short, sharp, speed section, where speeds of up to 20 kilometres per hour are required for a distance that is usually about four kilometres. As the going over this section is of major importance, course builders usually try to route it through country that is free from difficult gates or gradients. As most of the courses are closed to motor vehicles, the competitors usually walk this section to ensure that they are prepared for any twists and turns that they may have to drive at speed.

Reconnaissance is also essential for the hazards as each one will present a different problem and must be carefully considered. This is best done several times until you are absolutely sure of the route that you will take through it. It is a good idea for your groom to accompany you on these reconnaissances so that both of you know what you intend to do. You should draw a diagram of the hazard with your route clearly marked so that your groom can describe it to you as a reminder just before you get to it during the competition. Having decided on a course of action, it can be disastrous to change your mind when you reach the hazard, even though some gap suddenly seems more attractive. If you get stuck, it may be necessary to loop round to get a better line to a gate, but in doing so you must be very careful that you do not go through a lettered gate in the wrong order. A competitor is now deemed to be within the hazard area once he has passed through the entry gates and until such time as he passes through the exit gates. When doing your reconnaissance you should note the position of the exit gates carefully so that you do not have the hazard unintentionally.

The rules for hazards are the ones that seem to be the most liable to change so it is important to keep up to date, but at the time of writing it is possible to correct any mistake in a hazard by going back to the point at which the mistake was made and then driving the remainder of the

Fig 106 Jimmy Robson in a well-dressed hazard.

Fig 107 Louise Serjeant cornering at speed.

Fig 108 Dick Beeby at Sandringham in 1984.

Fig 109 George Bowman driving the James Dalton Seasoning & Spices team at Scone in 1985.

Fig 110 Mary Matthews at Wylye with Caesar and Cleopatra.

Fig 111 George Bowman in a hazard.

hazard correctly. If you have to do this you will collect 20 penalty points on top of the time penalties which you incur, but if a mistake is not corrected it will most probably result in your elimination. The penalty of elimination is very drastic and the decision for this rests with the President of the Ground Jury to whom recommendations are made by the obstacle judges.

The Groom's Role

Because the driver has so much to think about while driving the marathon, it is a definite advantage to have a reliable groom who not only knows the rules but also has a pretty good idea of what the driver is thinking. He must be ready to assist when required and must avoid taking unilateral action, allowing the driver to make all the decisions – be they right or wrong – because the success or failure of the drive must ultimately be his responsibility.

At the halts, the groom should attend to the horse or horses so that the driver can dismount from the vehicle and stretch his legs. With a bucket of water and a sponge, the groom can refresh the horse by sponging round his eyes and mouth and removing lather or sweat from around the collar, breeching and the horse's sides. It is a mistake to pour water freely over both horse and harness as this may cause the animal to become chilled while he is waiting to start the next section of the marathon, and he will not appreciate having cold, wet harness to work in.

When on the route the groom should keep a check on the time and advise the driver when to look for kilometre markers, if those have been placed on the course. He should also be looking ahead to warn the driver of marker arrows or obstructions on the course. In short, the groom should be another pair of eyes to assist the driver.

On section E, the groom should be able to warn the driver when he is approaching a hazard and, having previously walked round it and discussed it, be able to describe it and the route that the driver has decided to take. When in the hazard, the groom should keep quiet and allow the driver to concentrate, only offering advice if it is asked for. If it is necessary to make turns on a slope, the groom should know which way to lean in order to

Fig 112 Mark Broadbent tackles the Osberton water in 1984.

Fig 113 Claudia Bunn springing her team through a hazard.

Fig 114 Lt.-Col. Hywel Davies with the Household Cavalry team at Wylye in 1984.

'ballast' the vehicle properly. On no account should he get out of the vehicle unless asked to do so by the driver. Once a groom is down in a hazard he should stay down, even after he has sorted out the problem for which the driver asked him to dismount. He should be ready either to assist the driver again or resume his place on the carriage as it is about to leave the hazard. It is not necessary, as is sometimes mistakenly thought, for the groom to follow the route of the carriage through all the gates of the hazard.

The spares that are carried on the marathon should be easily accessible to the groom so that any necessary repairs or replacements to either harness or vehicle can be quickly and effectively carried out. He should also have a good, sharp penknife in his pocket at all times, as you never know when it might be needed.

Walking the Hazards

This is probably the most important piece of preparation that you have to do for an event and one that you obviously cannot do until you arrive. Once the course is declared open you should use any spare time to go and have another look at the hazards, because on a second, or even third, visit you may notice something that had escaped you previously.

The event organisers usually provide sketch maps of the hazards but these have varying degrees of accuracy and legibility so it is always best to take paper and pencil with you to correct, redefine or redraw the plan. You will also need to mark clearly the route that you intend to take, so that your groom can understand it and brief you before you get there (*see Fig 115*). Before walking into the hazard, take a good look at it to recognise

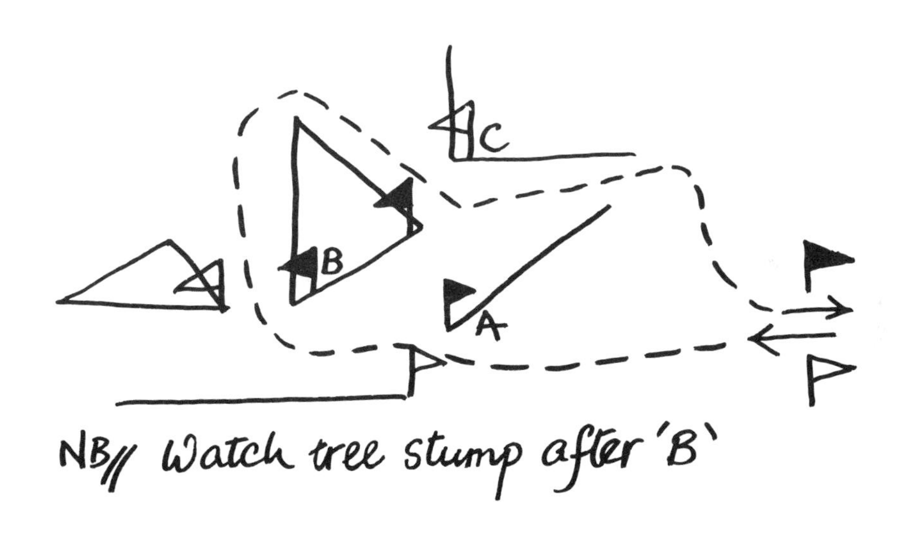

Fig 115 Plan of a hazard on which the competitor has planned his route and made notes.

where the gates are positioned and how they tally with the plan. Note where the entrance and exit gates are – they might well be one and the same as it cuts down the number of obstacle judges if they are – and the extent of the penalty zone. As you go through the entrance, heading towards gate A on the line that you think you can drive, you should already be looking for gate B to see if it is possible to take a straight line from one to the other. If it is not, you must work out the best line of approach once you are clear of the preceding gate. It is a good idea to carry with you a stout stick, cut to the same size as the track width of your vehicle, so that you can readily measure any gaps that might be a possibility. It may appear you have plenty of room but once you take a horse and carriage into a hazard it is surprising how much tighter the gaps turn out to be, so it is better to err on the side of caution than to be over-ambitious. Having decided on your best course of action you should then take a last look at the hazard and note any tree roots or large hummocks that are liable to tip your carriage at a crucial moment, or any overhanging branches that might snatch your whip out of your hand. These too should be noted on your hazard diagram so that your groom can remind you of them as you approach. The last note should tell you which way to turn on leaving the hazard, because in your excitement at having successfully negotiated it, vital seconds can be lost by turning the wrong way on to the route.

Driving with Two Hands

While it is advantageous on sections A, B, C, and D to drive your horse or horses with the reins held the conventional way in one hand, to give a balanced feel to each side of the horse's mouth, when you come to tackle the hazards of section E it is usually best to use two hands. This will enable you to turn your horses much more quickly and positively without losing the forward momentum that is so necessary. One thing to guard against is getting carried away with exuberance as you race for the exit gate and slapping the reins on the horse's backside like a western cowboy. The horse may not have seen the same film and might take violent exception to being treated in this way, modifying the front of your carriage with his two back feet.

For teams and tandems the usual practice is to buckle together the near side reins and to hold them in the left hand, whilst the off side reins are similarly buckled and held in the right hand. The adjustment should be such that while the wheelers are fully into their collars, you should have a light feeling on their mouths, and the leaders should at the same time be just held out of draft. This means that the wheelers will be doing the work in the hazards, but if there is a steep gradient to be tackled your leaders can be put into their work by letting your hands forward. Obviously by pulling the two reins on one side simultaneously there will be a tendency for the whole team to come over together, but this can be avoided by taking a loop in your leader rein and holding it under your thumb until the turn has been completed. Shallow turns and inclines can be obtained by rolling your wrists in opposite directions so that a pull on one side of the horses is compensated by a lessening of tension on the other. Although this may seem a very awkward form of driving at first, practice

Fig 116 Outside assistance is only allowed in case of an accident.

will prove that it can be very effective and useful.

Hazard Types

Every hazard is different and because each is specially built for an event there is little chance that you will have seen it before. There are a few basic guidelines that can be applied when driving specific types of hazard:

1. Post and rails – the most common building material for hazards. Builders tend to leave tempting gaps, but the turn into them must be considered carefully. Do not turn until the front of your wheel is past the post around which you are turning.
2. Water – spectacular hazards, but not usually too difficult if your horses have been schooled properly. The important thing is to get the horse into the water quietly and once he is in, just keep him moving.
3. Sand-pits – require strong horses, so if there is a sand-pit on the course make sure that your animal has plenty of energy left to get through it.
4. Slopes – where hazards are built on a slope, it is best to get well up before turning into a downhill gate, because the horse will drop down sideways more quickly than you anticipate.

10 Obstacle Driving

The last phase of a ridden three-day event is the showjumping, where the horses and riders who, the day before, have been galloping over a demanding cross-country course are tested for the suppleness and discipline that a jumping course requires. In driving events, the third day has a similar test of suppleness and discipline in the obstacle driving course which takes place in the arena and is designed to test the fitness of the horses after the marathon, as well as the skill of the competitor.

The idea is for the driver to negotiate a course between pairs of cones set 30–60 centimetres wider than the track width of his vehicle. For singles and pairs this allowance may sometimes be reduced to 20 centimetres, but under no circumstances is it to be more than 60 centimetres, nor may the track width of the carriage exceed 160 centimetres. For many years the varying width of carriages used in dressage and obstacle driving (for competitors must use the same vehicles in both phases of the event) made cone driving a very tedious part of the competition, as the pairs of cones had to be reset to meet the required track width of each vehicle. For this a double-ended slide rule was used so that the allowance could be set at one end and the vehicle track width at the other (*see Fig 117*). It was necessary to have one or two stewards to measure each vehicle beforehand and then relay this information to a large arena party whose job it was to set every pair of cones correctly before the competitor could drive the course. The whole procedure was expensive in both time and manpower and one of the great advances the sport made in Britain was the standardisation of track widths, which came into effect in 1985. This was made possible by permitting the use of scurry bars or 'hula hoops', two attachments

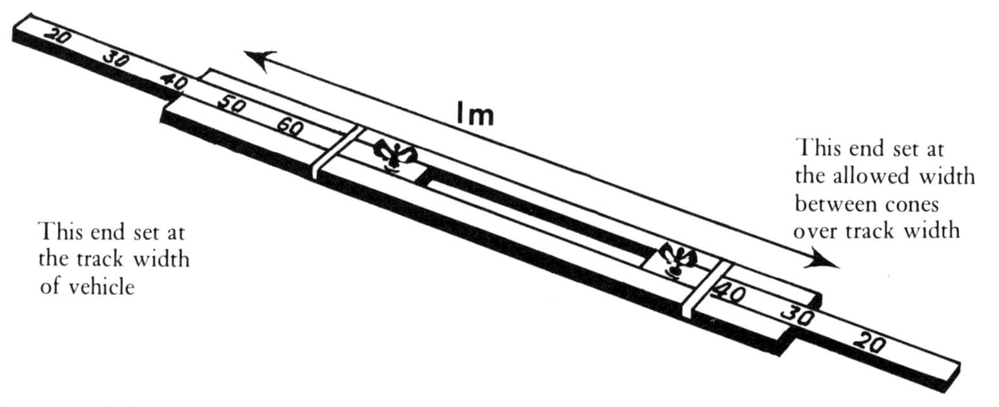

Fig 117 A slide rule for determining the distance between cones.

Fig 118 A vehicle fitted with a scurry bar.

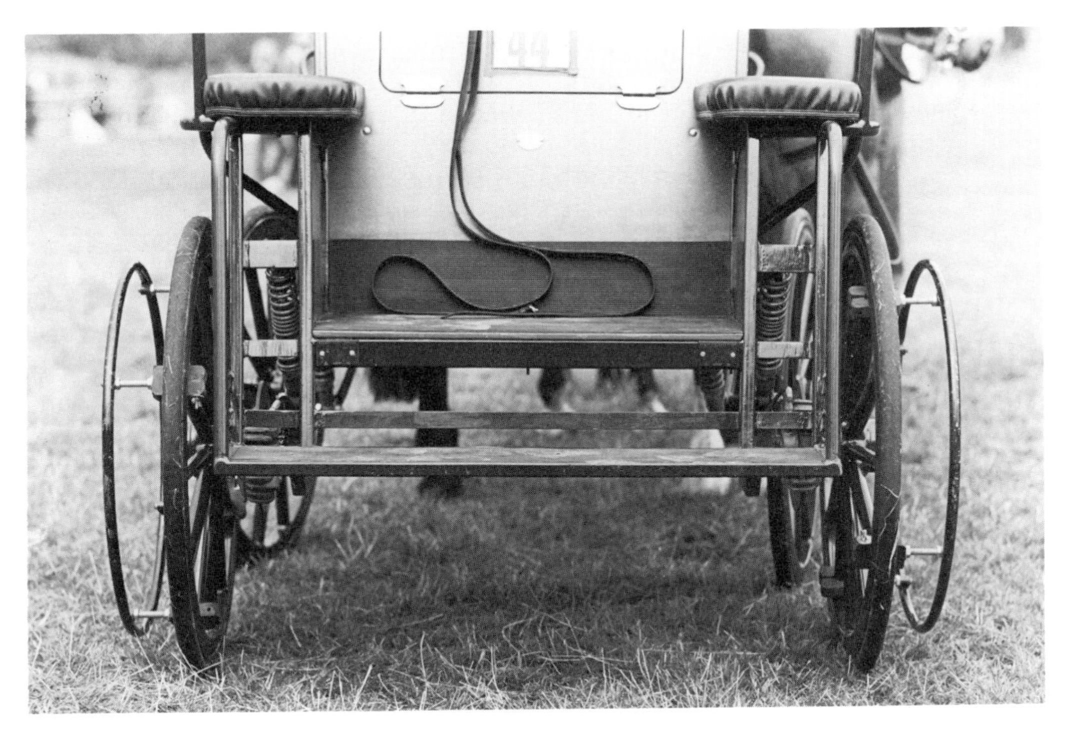

Fig 119 A vehicle fitted with hula hoops.

which can be fitted to carriages to bring them to the required width for the class in which they are entered. As a general rule these widths are 140 centimetres for ponies, 150 centimetres for horses and 160 centimetres for horse teams. By this one move, the whole competition was made much slicker and more attractive to spectators.

The course consists of a maximum of 20 obstacles, the majority of which are simply pairs of cones but these may be augmented by arrangements of jumping poles to form multiple obstacles. These multiple obstacles must not be longer than 30 metres (measured along the track the vehicle would take) and the length of the whole course is between 500 and 800 metres. It is designed to be a series of turns and circles arranged in such a way that it will be equally testing for all classes of competitors from single ponies up to horse teams. To make it more interesting, it may incorporate a bridge or a water crossing and the whole thing always looks much better when decorated with flowers and shrubs.

Types of Cones

Ever since competitive carriage driving started there has been one type of cone in constant use for national and international events, and that is the yellow triangular cone with a red disc on one side and a white disc on the other. It stands about 70 centimetres high, well over the prescribed minimum height of 30 centimetres, and has an upright leading edge of 10 centimetres which enables it to be used by vehicles with scurry bars or hula hoops. In the flat top there is a two-inch (5 cm) diameter hole, in which a ball is rested and it is when this ball is dislodged that penalties are awarded. In 1985 the firm that had been making these cones went out of production and as it would have been a very expensive exercise for another plastics manufacturer to set up the necessary mouldings, the driving world looked for a suitable alternative. A German manufacturer produced a conical cone made from a flexible plastic which was approved for international competition and was first used at Duerne in Holland in the spring of 1986. This was also the year that Great Britain hosted the World Four-in-Hand Championships at Ascot and a set of these cones was used there.

As there is no standard track width for international competition, these cones still had to be set for each individual carriage, which was fine under those circumstances but not suitable for competitions held under British national rules, where hula hoops were allowed. The sloping sides of these new cones meant that the track width could only be set at ground level, and as hula hoops were allowed to be 10 centimetres off the ground, competitors using them would have a distinct advantage. The problem was finally solved by a member of the Horse Driving Trials Committee, Jill Holah, who, after discussion with Michael Mart (the carriage builder who is well know for his inventive ideas), produced a cone which incorporated the old triangular cone and the new conical one, and which complied with both national and international requirements. The addition of small flaps on each side of the base gave it added stability, to help solve problems that had always arisen at windy venues where the other cones were used. Another advantage of these new cones is

Fig 120 Four types of cone.

that they are made of red plastic similar to the traffic cones through which so many people school their horses (*see Fig 120*).

Multiple Obstacles

These are usually built with jumping poles set on stands or cups in the top of traffic cones and are in the form of a U, an L, a box or dog-leg, and a slalom (*see Fig 121*). The measurements are specified in the rules, but generally the entrance must always be four metres wide with five metres width at a turn or exit. Once again, the parts of such obstacles are easily obtained or manufactured at home where your horse can be schooled through poles erected on cones or stands. This schooling is particularly important if you are driving a pony whom the children had previously used for gymkhanas, and who might get excited when confronted by the poles over which he used to leap.

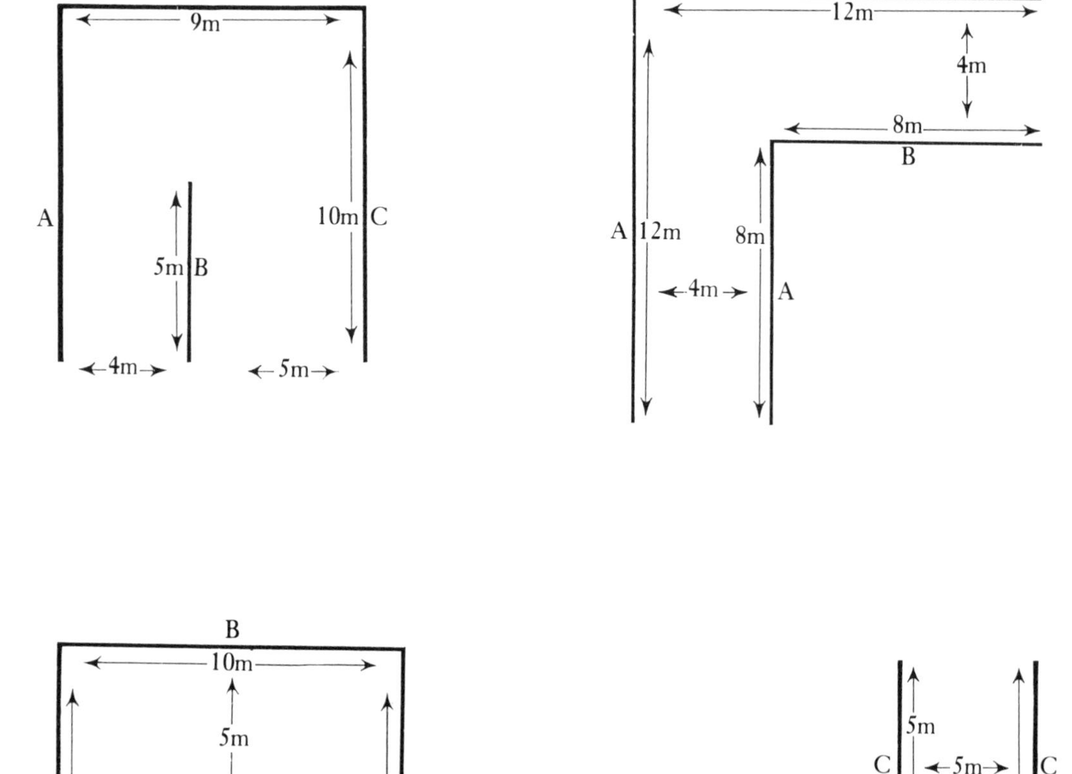

Fig 121 Multiple obstacles and their dimensions.

Judging and Scoring

Of all the phases of the competition, the cone driving requires a judge who is fully cognisant of the rules and can quickly spot any infringement. Based as it is on the showjumping competition, you will be penalised for a refusal, which includes stopping or backing in front of an obstacle or circling in such a way that you cross your own tracks. There are usually two judges sitting in the judging box together with a scorer, a commentator and someone to operate the timing equipment. One judge usually operates the bell to start the round and to stop it if necessary – whilst the other operates a stop watch as a back-up to the electric timing equipment, in case of a breakdown. The scoring is done on a card which again is similar to the cards used to judge showjumping (*see Fig 122*). The scorer usually has a master copy of the results of competitions A and B so that the cone driving scores can be quickly added on to give a complete overall result as soon as the class finishes.

Driving the Course

Time is always allowed for competitors to walk the course before their class takes place for essential reconnaissance. The

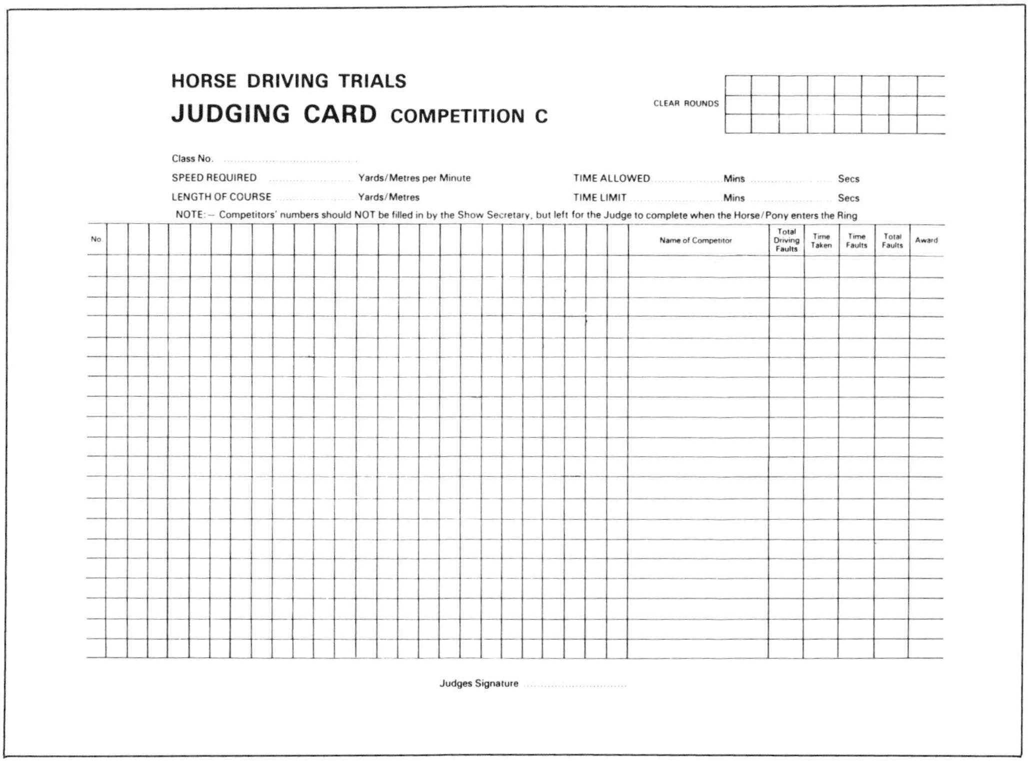

HORSE DRIVING TRIALS

JUDGING CARD COMPETITION C

CLEAR ROUNDS

Class No. ....

SPEED REQUIRED .... Yards/Metres per Minute TIME ALLOWED .... Mins .... Secs

LENGTH OF COURSE .... Yards/Metres TIME LIMIT .... Mins .... Secs

NOTE: – Competitors' numbers should NOT be filled in by the Show Secretary, but left for the Judge to complete when the Horse/Pony enters the Ring

No																										Name of Competitor	Total Driving Faults	Time Taken	Time Faults	Total Faults	Award

Judges Signature ....

Fig 122 Cone scoring card.

first thing to note is the route from entering the arena to where you will salute the judges and then move to face the start. Great care should be taken not to cross the start or finish line whilst doing this as that would render you liable for elimination. The number of each obstacle, be it pair of cones or multiple, should be clearly visible to you as you pass the preceding one and when walking the course you should go along the track that you intend to take so that not only can you check the visibility of the numbers, but also the best angle for tackling the obstacles. It may sometimes be necessary to turn away from an obstacle before approaching it to drive through it. In this case it is important that you do not cross your tracks as this can be construed as a refusal. Your groom may walk the course with you so that you can discuss it, but whilst you are actually driving the course the groom must remain seated and silent. If any groom is caught talking to the driver or pointing the way, immediate elimination ensues, but many grooms develop ventriloqual skills that would credit any music-hall stage.

Fig 123 Paul Gregory driving his black Welsh cobs at Floors.

Fig 124 Mark Broadbent at Holker Hall in 1984.

The same vehicle and harness must be used for this phase as was used for the presentation and dressage but with two differences. In Competition C your vehicle need not carry lamps and your horses may wear boots and bandages if you consider them necessary.

On entering the arena you should face the judges' box and salute in the correct manner. A gentleman does this by holding his reins and whip in his left hand and taking off his hat with his right hand. A lady should hold her reins in her left hand and salute by bringing her whip up in front of her face, holding it parallel to the ground and inclining her head forward in a polite nod. When driving tandems or teams with two reins in each hand, it is important to get your reins back into each hand correctly before starting the course. The signal for you to start is then given, usually by a bell or whistle, and you must pass the start line within one minute. A steady, even trot is the best pace at which to drive and you should then be able to get round in the time allowed, which is usually very generous. There may be long open stretches of the course that tempt you to canter but such speed is rarely necessary and only upsets your horse's balance and rhythm. A short sprint from the last obstacle to the finishing line is permissible, but only do it if you are confident that you can stop your horse once you have passed the post.

When this competition is the third phase of an event, it is judged by the number of faults that a competitor incurs. Sometimes, however, there is also a separate prize for this phase and in the event of equal scores the fastest time can decide the winner, or a run off can be held over a shortened course against the clock. This is then classed as a timed competition, and from this has developed the popular scurry driving competitions which are now such a feature of many major horse shows.

Scurry Competition

This is one part of the three-day driving event that has developed into a separate sport and has its own adherents who have concentrated on this alone and developed it into a definite style. There are only two classes, one for pairs of ponies under 12hh. and one for those pairs over that height, and although there is no limit, they rarely exceed 14hh. Shetland ponies are favourites in the former class because of their speed and sure-footed ability to turn quickly.

The vehicles have developed into a standard pattern within the rules laid down for this competition and have a minimum track width of 130 centimetres between the wheels which must not be pneumatic or wire-spoked. They are built with just two seats, one behind the other, for the driver and groom and are fairly low in order to keep the centre of gravity as near to the ground as possible. The course for these competitions is laid out using the same type of cones as in the three-day events, but only 12–14 gates, including one multiple in addition to the serpentine, are used in a large outdoor arena and these are reduced to 10–12 gates for smaller or indoor arenas.

11 Competition Organisation

Private Driving Classes

Where these classes are held as part of a larger horse show or agricultural show, there are a few points to which the show secretary should attend. If the show is affiliated to a national organising body, as most of them are, the secretary will have received guidelines as to what is required by driving competitors. Firstly there must be ample space for parking of horse boxes and carriage trailers and room for competitors to harness up and put to. If a ring is not available for an initial inspection, there should at least be some space for this if there is to be a marathon drive. The schedule should clearly state the divisions, if any, in the class and where prizes are to be awarded for various sections. Where classes are not divided it is best for the judge to send the larger horses around the ring first and the ponies afterwards so that the imbalance is not too marked. For the final selection they should all go around together and the judge will then indicate the order in which he has placed them.

All this requires good stewarding – an essential at any horse show – and choosing the right person for this job is most important. Whilst being a person who can organise and direct the competitors, the steward should not be too bossy, but firmly diplomatic. Neither should he try to give the judge his opinion as to the suitability of the competitors, because while he may think he is being helpful, he may be biased in favour of some competitors and the judge has been appointed as an impartial person. When inspecting a private driving class, the judge will look closely at the harness to ensure that it fits correctly and has been properly cleaned. The leather should be clean and supple and the brass buckles polished back and front. None of the buckles should be in the last hole, so that adjustment can be made in case of breakages.

The carriage should be of a proper size for the animal who is pulling it and should be clean and well painted. The age of the vehicle should not be a consideration as it is possible to turn out an old vehicle as smartly as a new one. If the harness has brass buckles, the fittings on the vehicle should also be in brass; similarly, silver-mounted harness must be complemented by silver carriage fittings. Lamps must be carried on the vehicle with used candles, not ones with fresh, unlit wicks. A comprehensive set of spares should be carried which should include a spare trace, rein, breeching strap and hame strap (if a full collar is used). A knife is essential, as is a strong leather bootlace or cord, and a bandage in case the horse or pony cuts a leg. A basic first-aid kit should also be included with the spares.

Having thoroughly inspected the class, the judge will ask the steward to get each turn-out to give an individual display before he sends them all round the ring for the final selection. The winners should be announced there and then, and the rosettes given out. If, for some organisational reason, the competitors are wanted back in the ring later in the day, it should be made clear to them exactly where and at what time they are required again.

If shows are in any doubt about the procedure for running private driving classes, they can always obtain help and advice from an official of the sport's governing body.

Horse Driving Trials

There are many aspects of organisation that go towards the running of a successful horse driving trials event. The actual location must be one of the most important, closely followed by the means to finance it and finding the right people for the many jobs that have to be done.

Location

Whilst the actual showground site may be contained within some 10–12 acres

Fig 125 Lt.-Col. Hetherington, organiser of many shows in the Midlands.

(4–5 hectares) the distance required for the five sections of the marathon is some 20–25 kilometres of roads and tracks, the last eight of which should be in close proximity to the main arena. This will allow the hazards to be sited where they can be easily seen by spectators who will not have to walk too far between each one. If the event is not being held on a large estate, as so many of them are, it is necessary to obtain the co-operation and help of neighbouring farmers and landowners over whose tracks the marathon will pass. The local police must also be consulted because they can give valuable guidance and help, particularly if the course crosses or uses any public roads. They can also advise on the routing to the event of competitors' horse boxes and spectators' cars.

Within the showground itself, the three main considerations should be the siting of the main arena, the stable area and the hazards of section E. If you anticipate having a large entry that will require two dressage arenas, you must also plan where the second one is to go. Both dressage arenas should be as flat as possible, devoid of nasty holes or bumps and be large enough to accommodate a 100 × 40-metre arena with a five-metre wide margin so that the judges' cars can be parked alongside it. The whole area should then be roped off to contain the large crowds of spectators you hope will attend.

The stable area is dictated to a certain extent by the number of days for which the event is to run. For a one-day event, where competitors are likely to arrive early in the morning but depart the same evening, there should be adequate parking space, but for a three-day event you will need a much larger site with plenty of room for caravans and temporary stabling. This will take up about five acres (2 hectares) and should have a hard road running through or alongside it so that lorries will not have to travel far on the soft grass. There should be an adequate supply of water, as well as places where competitors can empty manure and household rubbish. Mobile toilets should also be sited in the stable area, particularly if it is any distance from the main ring area where toilets are to be provided for the public.

In order to maintain control of the stable area and prevent chaotic parking, a stable manager should have a clearly marked caravan near the entrance where he can see every new arrival. Having been given a list of competitors, he can also check that they have brought the horses mentioned in their entry and can physically check them against their registration documents. The most important tool of the stable manager's trade is a large tractor which should be parked by his caravan to enable him to remove any horse boxes that may get bogged down, particularly if it rains heavily.

To keep the spectators interested and within controllable bounds, the hazards should preferably be located as near together as possible, with the course running from one to another in a 'clover leaf' fashion. This obviously depends to a large extent on the suitability of the ground, because for variety some slopes, banks and, if possible, water should be included.

Having decided where these three main areas are to be, it is possible to position the rest of the event. The secretary is the most sought after person by all and sundry and should be located in an office at the hub of things. Although he will have dealt with all the pre-show correspondence, it is advisable for him to have one or two assistants on the ground to deal with queries. At the larger events various duties can be delegated, such as dealing with competitors, trade stands, other main arena attractions and the public. The catering tent should also be a central feature so that it is easily accessible for spectators viewing at the main arena and for competitors from the stable area. Adequate toilets should be carefully sited where they are going to be easily accessible but will not constitute a health hazard. Modern mobile toilets are so efficient that they are well worth the extra expense that may be incurred. The scorers' caravan is another important office and ideally should be situated as close as possible to the dressage arenas and the finish of the marathon.

Planning

This is usually done by a small local committee headed by an experienced person who is in close touch with the Horse Driving Trials Events Committee. Whilst each member of the committee is delegated at least one task, they must all be concerned with the provision of that main essential – finance. The costs of running a three-day event may vary quite considerably, but can be huge, especially if the charges for using the estate are high. This money has to be found from various sources but it is always best if sponsorship can be raised from a large national company, preferably one with interests in your locality. For example, in Britain the Holker Hall event in Cumbria is sponsored by the Tetley Walker Brewery who sell their beer in that area; and although they operate on a greater nation-wide scale, the Norwich Union sponsor the Sandringham Driving Trials in their home county of Norfolk. Local tradespeople are often willing to purchase advertising space in your programme and sometimes may go as far as sponsoring a hazard or giving trophies and prize money for a particular class. Ringside banners are another source of income and these can also be used to 'dress up' hazards. The greater the monies raised by such commercial means, the better it will be for the competitors, as you will not only be able to give them improved facilities but will also be able to keep the entry fees down to a reasonable level. You should never lose sight of the fact that without competitors you have no event and as the cost of producing horses and carriages for competition is already very high, it is up to you not to burden the competitors more than necessary.

The appointment of officials for the event is done by the committee although the Technical Delegate and President of the Ground Jury must be appointed by the National Committee of Horse Driving Trials. It is usual to have a panel of three judges for each dressage class and if you are running two arenas, you will need four such panels. The Show Director, who is usually the chairman of the local committee, should liaise with the President of the Ground Jury as to which other judges should be invited. Obviously local judges will incur the least travel expenses, but it is as well to flavour the jury with a few imports from further afield.

The course builder is a very important choice and although there may be several enthusiastic amateurs who perform very well at club level, you must employ a person with national experience if you

Fig 126 The author takes time off from judging to keep his hand in with Lex Ruddiman's team at the end of an event.

are running a three-day event. Early consultation with the course builder will also give you a good idea of how much money you will need to spend on the hazards.

The recruitment of obstacle judges, timekeepers and referees used to be a major headache for the committee member who opted for this difficult task. Finding reliable people is never easy but the situation has been much improved of late with the formation of the Carriage Driving Supporters Club. This band of worthy people, who are keen to be involved in the sport but do not necessarily drive horses themselves, are willing and usually very able to act in one capacity or another at an event. The Secretary of the Supporters Club will liaise closely with the Event Secretary to provide any help and assistance that may be required.

From the moment that the competition begins there should be an efficient band of stewards who have been well briefed by the Show Director to assist in the smooth running of the event. While the Technical Delegate concerns himself with the progress of the actual competition, the Chief Steward is responsible for seeing that dressage and obstacle driving arenas are properly manned and that there is an efficient system for calling competitors forward when they are required. Where the collecting ring or presentation area is some way from the arena, walkie-talkie radio communication is a great help. If several of the stewards have these sets they will all know what is going on and will be ready to assist if a problem arises.

Local youth groups will often assist in the provision of an arena party and people to organise the selling of tickets at the gate, programmes and the parking of cars.

Speedy score collecting is the secret of obtaining fast results because, no matter how efficient your team of scorers may be, they cannot produce the end result without being fed the data from the timekeepers, obstacle judges and referees. The most satisfactory way of doing this is by pony club runners who need to be under the supervision of one or two adults. These useful people can then make sure that all points of the marathon course are covered and help the scorers by collating the paperwork as it comes in and sending for any missing sheets immediately. Motor cyclists also make good score collectors but sometimes tend to be somewhat dangerous amongst crowds of hazard spectators.

As the showground is likely to be populated for at least four days, a good firm of caterers should be obtained to provide meals and general refreshments. Some of these are also willing to sell milk and newspapers but if you have been warned that the firm you are using will not provide this service, local tradespeople should be asked to visit the stable area if possible.

Equipment

If you are running the event in conjunction with a local driving club, they will most probably already have some of the necessary equipment; if not, there are usually clubs from whom it can be obtained. The dressage arena is one of the biggest requirements and for this you want sufficient white boards to make two 100×40-metre arenas. Unless it is an international event, it is permissible to have the boards spaced out with gaps between them, but these gaps should be kept as small as possible. White sticks about a metre long are required as markers along the boards behind which the letters are placed. For the obstacle driving competition you will need a set of cones, the number of which can be calculated from the plan of your course. Jumping poles and stands, if you are intending to have a multiple obstacle, can often be borrowed from a local riding school. Electrical timing equipment is desirable and can often be provided by the firm that you employ to provide your communications and public address system. Clocks and watches are usually hired from the Horse Driving Trials Group.

All your honorary officials will appreciate some small souvenir of your event and a badge is usually enough to remind them of an enjoyable time spent at your horse driving trials. There are many excellent firms who will provide you with the badges and rosettes that you require, with your own choice of lettering and logo.

Timber and other materials for constructing marathon hazards will involve considerable expense but a clever course builder will make as much use as possible of natural features to keep the cost down. Posts and rope will be needed around the main arena at least, and you may find that it is also necessary to control the crowds around some of the hazards.

Waste skips must be placed in the stable area and these can usually be hired from a local firm, who may supply them just for advertisement. Remember that anyone who supplies a service cheaply or freely should be acknowledged in your programme. The hire of mobile toilets can be expensive but it is something that has to be done. The siting of these must be agreed with the owners of the land or their representatives, as large holes usually have to be dug. If at all possible, it is a good idea to have a public telephone installed and one for use in the secretary's tent.

Publicity

One point on which many shows fall short is publicity. You should contact a printer early in your preparations and get a good supply of posters and handbills which your committee can distribute as far afield as possible. As already mentioned, most, if not all, of the cost of your printing and publicity can be covered by getting local and national companies to buy advertising space in your programmes. Contact your local TV and radio stations who are usually only too willing to mention your forthcoming event in news of the local sports fixtures.

Officials

Show Director

This is usually a title accorded to the Chairman of the Show Committee, the person who shoulders the ultimate responsibility for the running of the event. He must be able to delegate the correct jobs to the right people so that everyone is occupied according to their abilities.

Technical Delegate

He is appointed to the event by the Committee of Horse Driving Trials and is responsible to them for the correct running of the event. In order that no unnecessary work is done, that may have to be changed, it is usual for the Technical Delegate to visit the course at intervals beforehand to see the course preparations and the building of the hazards. He must make sure that the course is going to be fair to all competitors and that local knowledge will not give an unfair advantage to some. He must also ensure that all the technical details are in accordance with the current rules. When he is satisfied that the course is ready, he will tell the President of the Ground Jury who is then usually taken round the course. The Technical Delegate is responsible for ensuring that all obstacle judges, timekeepers and referees are correctly briefed and whilst delegating some of this briefing to a senior judge, it is usual for him to do most of it himself. Even after handing the course over to the President of the Ground Jury, the Technical Delegate is still responsible for the technical conduct of the competition, although he should not be called upon to sort out any of the problems at the end of the marathon unless the President of the Jury asks for a specific technical question to be answered.

Judges

The President of the Ground Jury for any horse driving trial is appointed by the Horse Driving Trials Committee, but the remainder of the jury may be selected by the committee of the event from the current lists of official judges. The four lists are:

1. International judges.
2. National judges.
3. Associate judges (for singles and pairs only).
4. Probationary judges.

Except for those on the fourth list, who are still learning the job, all the people on these lists have been carefully selected for their suitability and competence to judge all phases of driving trials. Not only must they understand the national rules but be able to enforce them in a polite but firm way that does not offend competitors. A judge's personality is as vital as his knowledge of the sport and his integrity is as important as his intelligence.

Three judges are required to judge dressage tests at national events, and where there is a presentation section, at least one is required for that phase. It has become quite common practice to divide judges into panels of three and these panels judge both phases of competition

Fig 127 Miss Joan Harland, a national judge and frequent competitor.

A. However, this is not completely satisfactory for presentation as having to divide the small presentation scores by three leads to greater inaccuracy. The judging of competitions B and C is less demanding for judges whose duties are detailed by the President of the Jury. To judge the obstacle driving of competition C requires sharp eyes and an ability to make instant decisions in accordance with the rules.

Before the driving season starts each year, a judges' clinic is held to ensure that all judges are up to date with the latest changes to the rules and any grey areas are clarified so that they are all thinking and judging along the right lines. At the same time they undergo tests which are designed to show up any flaws in competence that can then be corrected. Driving trials could not run as well as they do without the dedication of people who have spent a great deal of time studying to become accepted as judges.

Hazard Judges

As the sport of competitive carriage driving has grown, so has the number of people who are required to run an event. From the early days, when one or two hazard judges were considered sufficient, it is now necessary to have four or five people to judge each hazard. Along with this increase in numbers has come an increase in experienced volunteers ready to assist in this capacity and with the help of comprehensive briefing, efficient teams of hazard judges are being produced. Even the competitors are beginning to acknowledge this professionalism and queries against hazard judges' decisions are becoming fewer. Whereas the competitor has eight hazards to remember, the hazard judges are only concerned with their one particular hazard and quickly become experts in their own specific area.

The timing of a hazard is extremely important because the competitor incurs penalties for every second that he is in the hazard. Although various electronic devices have been tried for this job, these are very expensive for the show and none has yet really proved reliable enough to dispense with a person with a stop-watch stationed at the gate to the hazard. The time is taken from when the horse's nose enters the hazard until he crosses through the gate on the way out. Usually the entrance and exit gates are one and the same but where they are different another person should be stationed at the exit to indicate to the timekeeper when the horse's nose passes the finishing line. As some competitors may find difficulty in negotiating the hazard, taking much more time than usual, it is necessary to have somebody with a stop-watch 50 yards (46 m) before the hazard to record hold-up times for any following competitors. This time is then recorded on the hazard judge's sheet and is sent to the scorers who deduct it from the competitor's time for section E.

Hazard judges have a sketch of their hazard for each competitor so that one of their group can record the route driven. This must be done by a continuous line marked on the sketch as the competitor actually drives it, and should not be left until he has gone through, as memory has a habit of being inaccurate on occasions. Supervising the hazard should be a hazard 'captain' who can fill the score-sheet and operate a radio to marathon control. On the score-sheet are several columns and these are only to be ticked if a competitor commits one of the misdemeanours listed in *Fig 128*. Otherwise, apart from the hazard details at the top of the page, all that has to be filled in is the competitor's number (taken from the number cloth his groom or referee is wearing and not from the running order) and the time he takes to drive the hazard, clearly defining the minutes or seconds. If the competitor is in the hazard for longer than five minutes, a whistle will be blown and he will be asked to leave as he will have exceeded the time allowed. This, or any other action which warrants elimination, is simply reported to the scorers who will in turn report to the President of the Jury for a final decision. It is not the duty of the hazard judges to inform the competitor of any possible elimination.

Apart from the people detailed above, it is always useful to have an extra person who can relieve any one of the group who may be in need of a break during a long day.

Course Builder

Although one person is usually appointed to build the course, he is supported by a team to help him with the actual construction of the marathon hazards, etc. As some of this team are locally recruited, their knowledge of the terrain and local contacts can be immensely helpful to a course builder who may be a stranger to the area.

The minimum width of gates in hazards is laid down at 2.5 metres but apart from that, the course designer can build any type of hazard which he thinks will

Horse Driving Trials **B.H.S.** **Obstacle Judge's Score Sheet**

FAULTS AT MARATHON OBSTACLES

Class No. .... Sheet No. ....

Obstacle No. .... Time Allowed .... Judge ....

Horse No.	(a) Putting down Whip	(b) First Groom Dismount	(c) Second Groom Dismount	(d) Driver Dismount	(e) Turning Over	(f) Leaving Penalty Zone	(g) Disconnect Traces	(h) Wrong Course	(i) Knock Down	(j) Time Taken
	20	10	20	30	60	20	Elimination	Elimination	10 per gate	

Fig 128 Hazard judges' scorecard.

be suitable for the event. His job is obviously most difficult if he has to pose problems for single ponies and still have a hazard that is drivable by horse teams, but the most experienced course builders seem to manage it.

There are two schools of thought on hazards – one that they should be open and free flowing and another that they should be tight, to test the driver's judgement or make him go the long way round. Against the free-flowing hazards is the view that they tempt competitors to go too fast and therefore invite accidents, and against the tight hazards is the argument that it is not good for spectators to see horses and carriages hung up in hazards. The course builder therefore really has the cards stacked against him which makes it even more praiseworthy when a course gets favourable comments from all sides, as it did at the World Championships at Ascot in 1986.

If the marathon is continually punctuated by calls for the course builder to repair hazards, either the design is wrong and competitors are having difficulty in driving them, or the building is too flimsy and they are being knocked down – or it may be a combination of both these faults. Sometimes there is a separate course builder for the obstacle course but more usually it is just another chore when the rigours of the marathon day are over.

Event Secretary

As in any well-run organisation, the efficiency of the Secretary has a great bearing on the success or otherwise of an event.

The Event Secretary may also be the Secretary to the Event Organising Committee, in which case he will be responsible for compiling with them the schedule early in the year and, if it is a national event, forwarding it to the horse driving trials office for inclusion in the omnibus schedule which is sent out to all members of the Horse Driving Trials Group. He must then invite the judges and scorers and arrange accommodation for them. Working at all times in close cooperation with the Technical Delegate, he must contact all voluntary helpers who will act as writers, arena stewards, score collectors, timekeepers, hazard judges, ground and mounted referees. Emergency cover from the police, doctors and vets must also be organised and as soon as a timetable is arranged these busy people must be given specific times at which they are required to attend.

When the entries start coming in, the Secretary must check them and record their receipt, keeping a careful check that the numbers received will fit into the proposed timetable. After the close of entries, the Secretary, with one or two other members of the organising committee, will ballot the entries for the running order and this is then typed out for inclusion in the programme. Having got a firm number of entries, he can apply to the horse driving trials office for the paperwork and numbers that will be required.

About fourteen days before the event, he must post badges, passes and any relevant information to all competitors, officials and helpers. In the week immediately prior to the event his work increases greatly and as the time limit for withdrawals passes, he can start to work out the presentation and dressage times. Working from the programme each class is split in half so that the bottom half do their presentation and dressage first and then revert to programme order for the marathon. The timings for the marathon are worked out by the Technical Delegate who will give them to the Event Secretary so that he can combine them with the other timings and produce the immense amount of copies that are always required. Once the event is under way, the Secretary must check well before the start of each class that he has the correct number of clipboards available, each with the proper paperwork on them, and can issue them to the writers who usually also need directing to their posts. As the event progresses, his main responsibility is the smooth running of the office and the control of clipboards, watches, whistles, etc. As the scores are compiled after the marathon he has to type out the running order quickly for the obstacle driving and may also be required to organise the final prize giving.

Scorers

These are very important helpers because if they do not get the results out correctly or quickly enough, discontent amongst the competitors will soon ruin an event. A team of two or three for the presentation and dressage phase should be increased to four or five for the marathon. Whilst it is preferable that they should all be competently numerate, it is essential that the chief scorer is quick at arithmetic and is familiar with the up-to-date rules of the Horse Driving Trials Group, and is given all the necessary information regarding timings, late withdrawals, etc.

The scorers should be accommodated in a caravan that is situated as near as is convenient to the end of the marathon and is out of bounds to competitors. They should be in radio or telephone contact with the commentator who can quickly summon the President of the Jury in the event of problems requiring his decision. A score-board writer should be attached to the scoring team so that results can be published as soon as they are available. For the obstacle driving, the chief scorer will appoint one of the team to sit alongside the judge and complete the judging card (*see* Fig 00). This is done whilst the competitor is driving the course and a final result can be broadcast as soon as the class is over. Notes on the system of scoring are sent to all driving clubs when they become affiliated to the Horse Driving Trials Group.

Stewards

Without an efficient team of stewards an event will quickly become disjointed and behind time. The team should be organised well in advance under the leadership of a competent person who is fully conversant with the requirements of a horse driving event; it is a good idea if he is also a member of the organising committee so that he is fully aware of all that is being planned. The Chief Steward should not be tied down to any one specific task, but should be free to rove around to ensure that his team is carrying out its duties satisfactorily. There should be one steward for each panel of presentation judges and two for each dressage arena.

On the marathon there is often a need for stewards to be located on road crossings, at halts and other points on the course where crowd control may be necessary. The Chief Steward should liaise with the Technical Delegate as to likely requirements on the day. Experienced stewards may also be employed as ground referees at points on the course where competitors may look for some advantage.

During the obstacle driving the stewards are needed to supervise the arena party and check the measurements of the cones, as well as to get the correct competitor into the arena when required for the cone driving and for the final prize givings.

Referees

There are two categories of referee – the ground referee and the mounted referee. The former is stationed at a strategic point on the marathon course where he can observe the competitors in the single horse and pony classes, the horse and pony tandem classes and the pony pairs class. Competitors in the horse pairs class and the horse and pony teams classes all have large vehicles on which they can carry a referee to watch their every move. Being a ground referee is obviously a more tedious task and one for which there is never a rush of volunteers, so event organisers often use the bribe of a mounted referee job next time for those who serve their apprenticeship as ground referees. In actual fact, the system of ground referees, if properly organised, can be much fairer because they can oversee all the competitors in a class whereas the mounted referee, whether he intends to or not, can become biased in favour, or against, the competitor with whom he is riding.

The task of the referees is to ensure that the competitor takes the correct route, passing through all the numbered flags and driving at the required pace for each section. Any breaks of pace in excess of five seconds must be noted on the referee's card and reported to the debriefing judge at the end of the marathon. He also keeps a check on the time taken for each section as a back-up check on the timekeepers on the ground. In many European countries where competitions are only held for horse teams, the referee also becomes the official timekeeper and is responsible for seeing that the competitor starts every section at the correct time. The referee must also make a note of any time that is lost due to any delays. This does not include being held up outside a hazard when that is recorded by the hazard judge. When in a hazard, the competitor is under the jurisdiction of the hazard judges and all that the referee has to do is to sit tight.

Refereeing is not for the faint-hearted and the element of danger that is allied to the excitement cannot be denied. However, competitors are bound to supply a safe and comfortable seat for their referee, who must wear a hard hat. Anyone who has sat alongside a team driver might add that an American footballer's face guard could be useful protection from the whip, but things can be taken too far!

All referees are briefed on their duties by the Technical Delegate, usually the day before the marathon, and if time and the state of the course allow it, they may be taken around so that they can familiarise themselves with the location of the starts of sections, finishes and turning flags.

Timekeepers

Positioned at the beginning and end of every section of the marathon, the timekeepers are equipped with digital clocks, timekeeping books and a copy of the marathon running order. While running continuously, the clocks have a button by which the time may be frozen when a competitor crosses the line. All timing is taken as the horse's nose reaches the line in a similar fashion to the photo finish mechanism on racecourses. The time is then recorded in the timekeeper's book, the top pages of which are torn out and sent to the scorers whenever a runner comes to collect them. It is important that the timekeepers do not write down the competitor's number until they actually see it because so many things can happen on a long marathon that overtaking can, and frequently does, occur.

Those supervising the start of any section must ensure that the competitor starts from the halt with the horse's nose as close to the line as is practical. All the competitors carry time cards and these must be correctly filled in and initialled by the timekeepers before being handed back to the competitors. These cards are handed to the debriefing judge at the end of the marathon and enable the scorers to produce provisional results which are later checked against the timekeepers' sheets.

All officials on duty for the marathon must stay within earshot of the public address system until officially released by the President of the Ground Jury.

12 Travel and Accommodation

Anyone who has ever been to a carriage driving event must be full of admiration for the ingenuity shown by competitors in respect of the transport and living arrangements for their entourage and their horses. There are obviously degrees of difficulty in this, ranging from transporting a single pony and trap to a one-day show or event to the ultimate transporting of a full horse team with two vehicles and a complete team of helpers for a full three-day driving trial.

Transporting the Carriage

The most economical form of transport that can be used for single ponies, single horses, or horse and pony tandems is a horse trailer behind a pick-up truck. The vehicle can be quite easily loaded on to the back of the truck with its shafts over the roof of the cab and the boxes containing the harness carried underneath it, along with the forage requirements according to the length of your stay, your stable equipment and your luggage, all of which you can cover with a waterproof sheet.

Protecting the vehicle is a more difficult proposition and it is not really feasible unless you have a tailor-made cover for it. Wrapping it in a sheet is never very successful because the wind will cause it to flap and either that, or the cord securing it, is liable to damage the paintwork. Transporting the vehicle without protection means that you may have extra cleaning to do on it when you arrive at the event, but there will not be paintwork to be touched up. When securing the vehicle to the pick-up you should always attach the ropes to metal parts, for example the axle and steps, and never around the spokes or felloes of the wheels. The shafts will obviously have to be tied down and this is best done just in front of the tug stops for, if any marking is caused, it is less likely to be seen when the tugs are in-place. All points of the vehicle to which ropes are attached should be protected by a pad of material and the most suitable for this purpose is a strong cord cloth.

Transporting the Horses

Many singles and tandem competitors use a small horse box as opposed to a trailer. There are many permutations for loading into a horse box. A side ramp as well as a rear ramp is more convenient, as it means the horses can be loaded before or after the vehicle, whichever you find most practical. However, if your lorry is only blessed with a rear ramp, you will have to load the vehicle first and the horses last, so that they can be quickly released in an emergency. (For methods of loading singles, tandems and teams in Luton van types of horse box, *see Fig 129.*)

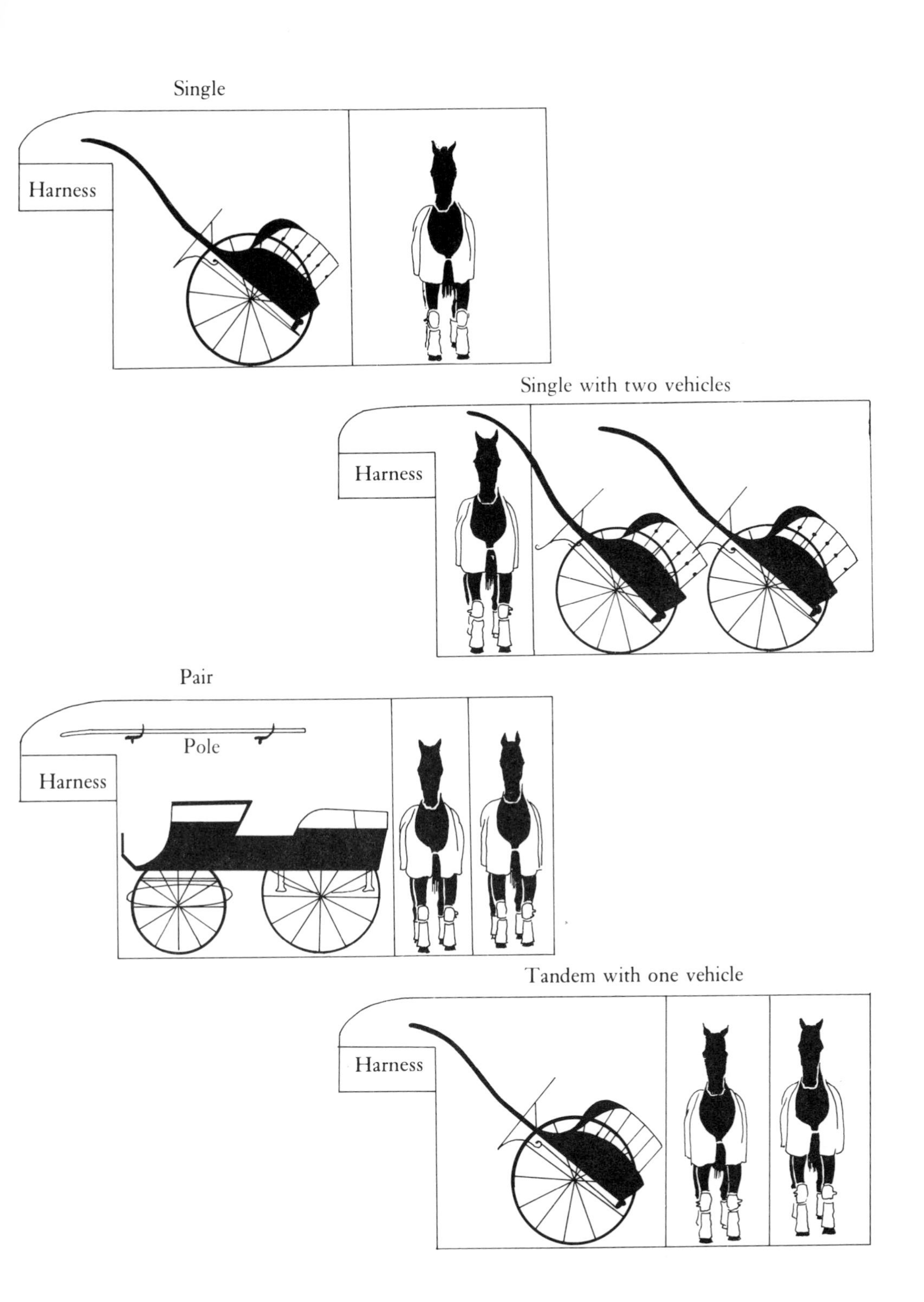

Fig 129 Various horse-box loads.

Some of the more unusual ways of loading are not shown here; for example, the pony tandem driver who had a vehicle strapped on to the front of his lorry on a frame that incorporated an extra set of headlamps. He has not appeared recently so perhaps the Law thought that that was taking things a little too far!

Horses and ponies travel best sideways or on an angle because this puts less strain on their legs than when they are facing forwards. Whilst not being cramped, they should nevertheless be in fairly narrow stalls that are strong enough to support them when they lean against them. If the stalls are too wide, the horses will be thrown around too much, and half a ton of horse flesh thrown against a partition from a distance of only 18 inches (45 cm) can do a lot of damage – to the box as well as to the horse.

Much of the animal's comfort depends on the way the vehicle is driven, be it a lorry or a car towing a trailer. Good anticipation is essential so that you can slow down in plenty of time without throwing your precious cargo about and causing damage and discomfort. If you are towing a trailer, be it one with horses in behind your car, or with carriages on behind your horse box, you must make sure that it is in good working order. The coupling must operate freely and be capable of being locked on to the towing vehicle. A safety chain or steel cable should also be attached to the towing vehicle so that if the coupling parts, as it sometimes does with sheer metal fatigue, the trailer will not go careering off on its own and cause untold damage. The lights should work correctly when plugged into the car or lorry – gone are the days when a well-known jobmaster relied on red bicycle lamps tied to the backs of his trailers – and correct trailer boards must now be used; these can be made or purchased relatively cheaply.

Temporary Stabling and Accommodation

As the charge for stabling at shows can be high, and the usual number of nights for which you will need it is four, the cost becomes quite prohibitive, particularly for those with several horses. It therefore makes sense to carry your own portable stabling with you. Although the initial outlay may seem a lot, you will have recouped that after only two or three events.

There are various styles of stabling, all usually made by competitors or their friends because no entrepreneur has yet floated a company for the manufacture of a particular design. Steel box section is the most popular material for the framework as it can be readily assembled with the pre-drilled holes for nuts and bolts. Partitions between horses can just be a 'swinging bale' of 1½-inch (3.75 cm) diameter round pipe, but a better idea is a board of half-inch (1.25 cm) ply measuring 8 feet (2.4m) by 2 feet 6 inches (75cm), suspended on chains about a foot (30cm) from the ground. Another important use for plywood is as a 'skirt' to fix along the side of the lorry. This serves two purposes – first, it stops horses trying to graze under the horse box and catching their headcollars on any projecting bolts and, second, it will insulate the stabling from wind blowing under the horse box.

The usual covering for temporary stabling is canvas, which must be se-

Fig 130 A smart temporary stabling set-up attached to Helen Sledge's horse box.

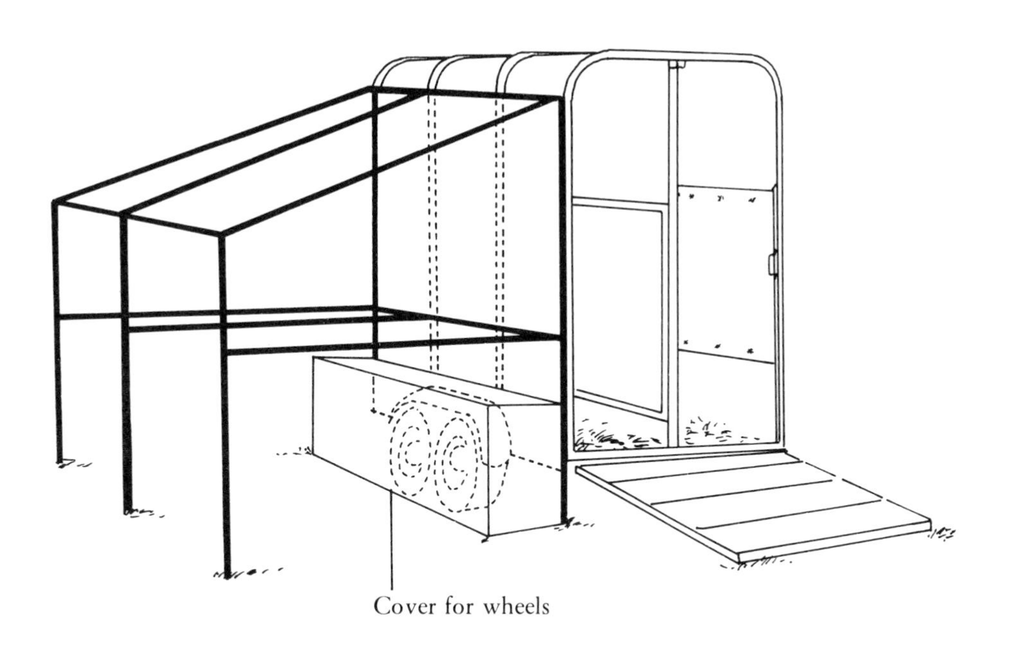

Fig 131 A trailer with temporary stabling.

Fig 132 The Holah family set-up, showing caravan, horse box and ponies in temporary stabling off a trailer.

curely tied down to prevent it from flapping or completely taking off. Its main disadvantage is the difficulty of putting it up, particularly in windy conditions, but it has the advantage of being easy to pack and store in some corner of your transport. There have been several experiments with metal or wooden roofs for temporary stabling, that are hinged to the side of the lorry, but these add to the weight and require several strong men to erect them. When in position, however, they are much more substantial than their canvas counterparts and give better protection from variable weather.

The horse trailer requires a few modifications for the temporary stabling which you plan to attach to it and once you have built this at home it is a good plan to let your animals spend a night in it so that not only do they get used to it, but you can see what alterations are required before it is put into use. Rings to which the horses can be tied should be firmly fixed to the side of the trailer and reinforced on the inside. One essential point is to make sure that the legs at each corner of the trailer are in good working order because these so often get bent and will not slide easily in their mountings.

Where do you sleep? Why, in the trailer, of course. If kept clean before the horses are loaded and cleaned as soon as they are unloaded, it can be made into a comfortable extemporary caravan. If there are more of you than it can accommodate, you will need an additional tent. Do not let anyone sleep in the front of the truck because if you are to get the maximum result and enjoyment from your weekend, everyone must be comfortable.

This book has covered the basic requirements that will help you in a successful and, above all, enjoyable career in carriage driving. None of us can say that we know it all and there are always aspects of the sport about which we can learn more, but I hope that these pages will prove to be of practical assistance to your driving.

Useful Addresses

The British Driving Society
Executive Secretary: Mrs J. Dillon
27 Dugard Place
Barford
Warwick
CV35 8DX

The British Horse Society
Horse Drving Trials Group
Secretary
Manor Farm
Bascote
Nr Leamington Spa
Warwickshire
CV33 0DX

Tel: 01926 815206
Fax: 01926 815173

The American Driving Society
Box 1852
Lakeville
Connecticut 06039

Fédération Equestre Internationale
Schloss Haldenstrasse 32
PO Box 3
CH 3000
Berne 32
Switzerland

Further Reading

HRH The Duke of Edinburgh *Competition Carriage Driving* (Horse Drawn Carriages Ltd, 1982)

Coombs, Tom *Horse Driving Trials* (David & Charles, 1985)

Walrond, Sallie *The Encyclopaedia of Driving* (Country Life Books, 1979)

Watney, Marilyn and Kenward, William *Show Driving Explained* (Ward Lock Ltd, 1978)

Ryder, Tom *On The Box Seat* (Horse Drawn Carriages Ltd, 1969)

MacDonald, Janet W. *The Right Horse* (Methuen, London, 1982)

The Duke of Beaufort *The Badminton Library Driving* (Ashford Press Publishing, 1986)

Velstra, Tjeerd *The Driving Horse and His Schooling* (Iska-Verlag 1988)

Index